Trends in Earnings Loss from Disabling Workplace Injuries in California

The Role of Economic Conditions

Robert T. Reville

Robert F. Schoeni

Craig W. Martin

Prepared for the
California Commission on Health and Safety and Workers' Compensation

The research described in this report was sponsored by the California Commission on Health and Safety and Workers' Compensation. This research was conducted by RAND's Institute for Civil Justice.

ISBN: 0-8330-3080-9

Published 2002 by RAND
1700 Main Street, P.O. Box 2138, Santa Monica, CA 90407-2138
1200 South Hayes Street, Arlington, VA 22202-5050
201 North Craig Street, Suite 102, Pittsburgh, PA 15213
RAND URL: http://www.rand.org/
To order RAND documents or to obtain additional information, contact Distribution Services: Telephone: (310) 451-7002; Fax: (310) 451-6915; Email: order@rand.org

THE RAND INSTITUTE FOR CIVIL JUSTICE

The mission of the RAND Institute for Civil Justice (ICJ) is to improve private and public decisionmaking on civil legal issues by supplying policymakers and the public with the results of objective, empirically based, analytic research. The ICJ facilitates change in the civil justice system by analyzing trends and outcomes, identifying and evaluating policy options, and bringing together representatives of different interests to debate alternative solutions to policy problems. The Institute builds on a long tradition of RAND research characterized by an interdisciplinary, empirical approach to public policy issues and rigorous standards of quality, objectivity, and independence.

ICJ research is supported by pooled grants from corporations, trade and professional associations, and individuals; by government grants and contracts; and by private foundations. The Institute disseminates its work widely to the legal, business, and research communities, and to the general public. In accordance with RAND policy, all Institute research products are subject to peer review before publication. ICJ publications do not necessarily reflect the opinions or policies of the research sponsors or of the ICJ Board of Overseers.

BOARD OF OVERSEERS

California Commission on Health and Safety and Workers' Compensation

Appointed by the Governor of California

Jill A. Dulich, Marriott International, *representing employers*

Leonard C. McLeod, California Correctional Peace Officers Association, *representing labor*

Darrel "Shorty" Thacker, Bay Counties District Council of Carpenters, *representing labor*

John C. Wilson, Schools Excess Liability Fund, *representing employers*

Appointed by the Speaker of the California Assembly

Allen Davenport, Service Employees International Union California State Counsel, *representing labor*

Robert B. Steinberg, Law Offices of Rose, Klein and Marias, *representing employers*

Appointed by the Senate Rules Committee

Tom Rankin, California Labor Federation, AFL-CIO, *representing labor*

Kristen Schwenkmeyer, Gordon and Schwenkmeyer, *representing employers*

Executive Officer

Christine Baker

Blue-Ribbon Permanent Disability Policy Advisory Committee

Co-Chairs

Tom Rankin, CHSWC and California Labor Federation, AFL-CIO

John C. Wilson, CHSWC and Schools Excess Liability Fund

Members

Rea B. Crane, R.N., C.D.M.S., C.C.M., Medical Rehabilitation, California Workers' Compensation Institute

Dominic Dimare, California Chamber of Commerce

Richard P. Gannon, Division of Workers' Compensation

Brian Hatch, California Professional Firefighters

D. Allan MacKenzie, M.D., Department of Industrial Relations, Industrial Medical Council

Suzanne P. Marria, Department of Industrial Relations Directorate

Theresa Muir, Southern California Edison

Michael Nolan, California Workers' Compensation Institute

Dianne Oki, State Compensation Insurance Fund

Merle Rabine, Workers' Compensation Appeals Board

Larry Silver, Esq., California Applicants' Attorneys Association

PREFACE

The Commission on Health and Safety and Workers' Compensation (CHSWC) is charged under the 1993 California workers' compensation reform legislation with conducting a continuing examination of the state's workers' compensation system. The adequacy and cost of benefits for permanent disability from occupational injuries is a source of controversy among policymakers in California. Out of concern about the adequacy of benefits for workers with permanent disabilities, the California legislature passed benefit increase bills in 1999, 2000, and 2001. But because of the cost of these increases, all three bills were vetoed.

In response to public opinion that was revealed at a fact-finding hearing in 1996, the CHSWC decided to undertake a multiyear review of the adequacy, equity, and cost of workers' compensation permanent disability benefits. Through a competitive bidding process, the RAND Institute for Civil Justice was selected to provide analyses to support this review. This report is the third produced by RAND for the CHSWC as part of this review. The others in the series are *Compensating Permanent Workplace Injuries: A Study of the California System* (Peterson et al., RAND MR-920-ICJ) and *Permanent Disability at Private Self-Insured Firms: A Study of Earnings Loss, Replacement, and Return to Work for Workers' Compensation Claimants* (Reville et al., RAND MR-1268-ICJ).

The CHSWC permanent disability project was designed to introduce improvements to the workers' compensation system that are rigorously supported by research, are mutually beneficial to employers and labor, and are agreeable to the system's stakeholders. In collaboration with stakeholders and through objective research, this project identifies problems within the workers' compensation system and builds a consensus on feasible policy changes in response to the research and analysis.

For the first phase of this project, the CHSWC commissioned RAND to evaluate permanent disability benefits. In two previous reports, RAND evaluated the adequacy and equity of benefits in the early 1990s. Peterson et al. (1998) examined benefits at insured firms, and Reville et al. (2001) examined benefits at self-insured firms. Both of these reports found evidence that benefits were inadequate in California. However, an advisory board to the CHSWC has suggested that improvements in the economy and in workers' compensation since the early 1990s have also improved outcomes for permanent disability claimants. This report tests that hypothesis by examining the changes in earnings losses for permanent disability claimants over the 1990s.

For more information about the Institute for Civil Justice, or for answers to questions on material contained in this report, contact:

Robert T. Reville, Acting Director
RAND Institute for Civil Justice
1700 Main Street
Santa Monica, CA 90407-2138
TEL: (310) 393-0411 x6786
FAX: (310) 451-6979
Email: Robert_Reville@rand.org

A profile of the ICJ, abstracts of its publications, and ordering information can be found on the World Wide Web at http://www.rand.org/centers/icj.

For further information about the CHSWC, contact:

Christine Baker, Executive Officer
California Commission on Health and Safety and Workers' Compensation
455 Golden Gate Ave., 10th Floor
San Francisco, California 94102
TEL: (415) 703-4220
FAX: (415) 703-4234
Email: chswc@dir.ca.gov
Web: http://www.dir.ca.gov

CONTENTS

FIGURES

TABLES

SUMMARY

A California worker who continues to have a permanently disabling condition after recovering from a workplace injury is entitled to permanent partial disability (PPD) benefits. In 1996, the California Commission on Health and Safety and Workers' Compensation (CHSWC) began a multiyear review of the PPD program to determine its effectiveness. This report, as part of that investigation, focuses on the economic consequences of disabling injuries in the 1990s and what those economic outcomes suggest about the adequacy of workers' compensation in California.

An earlier RAND study (Peterson et al., 1998) showed that workers injured on the job in 1991 at insured firms in California suffered significant and sustained wage losses, as well as low replacement rates for lost income, during the five years following injury. An advisory committee to the CHSWC argued that these results might have been partly driven by poor economic conditions in California during the early 1990s.

This report summarizes our investigation into the relationship between earnings losses and economic conditions in California during the 1990s. As part of our study, we used a model that was developed for analyzing the impact of economic conditions. We then extrapolated from the model's estimates to provide predictions of long-term (five- and ten-year) wage loss and replacement rates for workers injured from 1991 to 1997.

We found that changes in economic conditions have some impact on losses experienced by PPD claimants. However, such changes do not explain much of the general decline in earnings losses by claimants during the study period. That trend may be more closely related to conditions in the workers' compensation market in the early 1990s.

Our results concerning long-term outcomes indicate that the replacement rates for five-year losses for PPD claimants improved during the mid-1990s, but remain below 60 percent of pre-injury earnings. Replacement rates for ten-year losses are lower yet; those rates remain below one-half of pre-injury earnings. These estimates suggest that while benefit levels have increased since 1991 and earnings losses have declined, replacement rates still remain below the two-thirds wage-replacement standard commonly cited for adequacy. Because benefits have declined (in inflation-corrected dollars) since their last nominal increase in 1996 and, as of late 2001, the economy has headed into a new recession, it is possible that workers injured today will have worse outcomes than workers injured at the end of our observation period in 1996 and 1997.

STUDY APPROACH

To determine wage loss and replacement rates, we compared the earnings of injured workers with the earnings those workers would have received if their injuries had not occurred. Such workers recover a portion of their earnings in the years following their return to work, but a *wage loss* gap always remains. The portion of that loss that is replaced by workers' compensation benefits is the *replacement rate.*

Because we cannot observe what the injured worker would have earned in the absence of injury, we estimate earnings losses by using a matched comparison group. The comparison group consists of individuals working at the same firm as the injured employee who are also receiving the same wages. Both the injured workers and the controls are followed over the years after injury, and wage loss is measured as the difference between an injured worker's earnings and the average earnings of that person's comparison workers.

Because earnings data were available only through 1998, we cannot observe five-year earnings losses of workers injured after 1993. To estimate outcomes for workers injured more recently, we rely on a multivariate model that relates earnings losses to the severity of injury, local economic conditions, and other factors. The model is estimated using data on workers injured in 1991 to 1995, and includes data on workers at both insured and self-insured employers.[1] Besides controlling for the employment growth rate (which we used to measure economic conditions), and controlling for industry, severity of injury, and pre-injury earnings, we allowed the effect of severity and pre-injury earnings to differ with the year of injury. We also allowed the effect of a disabling injury to differ for self-insured and insured claimants in each year.

CHANGES IN ECONOMIC CONDITIONS AND THEIR EFFECTS ON INJURED WORKERS

Wage losses for injured workers may be particularly high when the economy is weak, as it was in California between 1991 and 1993. During difficult times, employers may be reluctant to find modified work for injured workers, making it more likely that such employees will lose their jobs. Also, other firms may be less likely to hire an injured worker when unemployment is high and nondisabled workers are available.

A look at changes in PPD claims from the recession year of 1991 to the post-recession year of 1995 shows significant improvements in outcomes. To discover if such results are related

---

[1]Instead of purchasing insurance for workers' compensation, employers may insure themselves for the costs of indemnity, medical compensation, and vocational rehabilitation following workplace injuries. To qualify, firms must meet stringent financial requirements. Therefore, those firms that qualify as self-insured employers are typically larger than insured firms are.

to better economic conditions in California, we examine the importance of economic conditions in three ways. First, we look at data for the whole state to see if the time pattern of earnings loss rises and falls with economic conditions. Second, we determine whether workers in counties with better economic conditions tend to experience lower earnings losses. Third, we examine the impact of economic conditions using a multivariate model that controls for other factors, such as severity of injury, that may have also changed from the recession year to the post-recession year.

The evidence in all three contexts suggests that economic conditions partially determine long-term outcomes for injured workers. In the 1991 to 1995 period, the effect of changing economic conditions was greatest for the least severely disabled claimants. Not only were those workers more likely to have better outcomes as economic conditions improved, but the overall decline in their wage losses and the improvement in their replacement rates were larger than those for workers with more-severe disabilities. By contrast, the most-disabled claimants experienced no changes in outcomes, and may have even lost some ground over the same period.

However, the large improvement in outcomes for less-disabled claimants cannot be explained by economic conditions alone. Our findings suggest that the earnings losses in the early 1990s reflected the impact on workers of a workers' compensation system in crisis. As firms were overwhelmed with claims, the ability to adequately accommodate injured workers may have been compromised. Since that time, in response to increased insurance rates, firms have adopted procedures to facilitate return to sustained work, a move that may have contributed to improvements in wage replacement rates for the least severely injured workers because those employees are most easily accommodated by return-to-work programs. Furthermore, workers' compensation reform legislation in 1993 raised benefits for temporary disability and some permanent disability claims. As these increased benefits were phased in from 1993 to 1996, average benefits increased faster than the rate of inflation, at least through 1996. The combination of declining earnings losses and increasing benefits resulted in improved outcomes for injured workers over this time period.

PREDICTED WORKERS' LOSSES

Looking at outcomes over five and ten years, and predicting the losses for PPD claimants by using data on benefits from 1991 to 1997, we find that benefits in California in 1997 were still below the two-thirds-of-pre-tax-losses replacement rate that is the usual standard for judging the adequacy of workers' compensation programs.

When evaluating PPD benefits, it is unclear over what time period the two-thirds standard is meant to apply—five years, ten years, a lifetime, or some other period? If the period is ten years, California falls far short of the two-thirds wage-replacement standard, not even achieving a one-half replacement rate. If the standard is five years, California still has inadequate benefits, although between declining wage losses and increasing benefits, over the 1990s, the system moved closer to meeting the standard of adequacy.

SEVERE DISABILITIES AND THE AMERICANS WITH DISABILITIES ACT

A surprising result of our study is that those workers with the most severe disability claims experienced no improvement over the period in question. This finding is unexpected because it was higher-rated claims that were targeted for benefit increases in the 1993 workers' compensation reform legislation. These results are consistent with a growing literature (unrelated to workers' compensation) that has found that severely disabled individuals experienced declines in employment during the 1990s. This trend is surprising given that severely disabled individuals were expected to benefit from increased civil rights protection from enforcement of the 1990 Americans with Disabilities Act.

ACKNOWLEDGMENTS

We are grateful to the members of the Commission on Health and Safety and Workers' Compensation for their support of this research. We would also like to express our thanks to Christine Baker, the Executive Director of the Commission, for her enthusiasm, assistance with access to the stakeholder community, and valuable comments. In addition, we thank the members of the CHSWC Permanent Disability Advisory Group, whose comments, criticism, questions, and research advice have been extremely helpful.

We are grateful for the support of the California Department of Industrial Relations (DIR) and its Director, Stephen Smith. In addition, we would like to thank Suzanne Marria, the Assistant Director of the DIR for her support and insightful comments.

We thank the California Workers' Compensation Insurance Rating Bureau (WCIRB) and the Employment Development Department (EDD) for their data. Dave Bellusci, of the California WCIRB, has been consistently helpful and accessible for questions and other assistance. At EDD, Rich Kihlthau was very helpful, managing our access to the data, and providing helpful comments and documentation.

Frank Neuhauser (University of California, Berkeley) and Jay Bhattacharya (Stanford University) provided formal comments that improved the document considerably. Sue Polich provided excellent programming support. We have benefited from the comments and ideas of Les Boden (Boston University), Jeff Biddle (Michigan State University), and Guido Imbens (UCLA). In addition, the members of the Workers' Compensation Research Group provided excellent comments and suggestions.

We thank Joanna Nelsen for her assistance throughout the project, and for formatting the document, and Nancy DelFavero for the excellent editing work on the final report.

Any errors that remain are our responsibility.

ACRONYMS

ADA	Americans with Disabilities Act
CHSWC	Commission on Health and Safety and Workers' Compensation (California)
DIR	Department of Industrial Relations (California)
EDD	Employment Development Department (California)
PPD	Permanent partial disability
TTD	Temporary total disability
WCIRB	Workers' Compensation Insurance Rating Bureau (California)

CHAPTER 1

INTRODUCTION

In California, a worker who suffers a workplace injury is entitled to permanent partial disability (PPD) benefits if, after recovery from the injury, the worker continues to have a disabling condition that will reduce his or her ability to compete in the open labor market. This benefits program is part of the state's workers' compensation system, which also provides temporary total disability (TTD) benefits (on a no-fault basis) while the worker is out of work recovering from a workplace injury, medical care, and vocational rehabilitation. In 1996, the California Commission on Health and Safety and Workers' Compensation (CHSWC) began a multiyear, comprehensive review of workers' compensation permanent partial disability. This report investigates trends in the economic consequences of a disabling injury during the 1990s and the implications of those trends for the adequacy of workers' compensation in California.

The analysis in this report was conducted in response to comments from stakeholders on an earlier report (Peterson et al., 1998), which showed that workers injured on the job in 1991 at insured firms in California experienced significant and sustained wage losses, as well as low replacement rates, over the five years immediately after injury. An advisory committee to the CHSWC argued that the results might have been driven in part by poor economic conditions in California during the early 1990s. As the economy improved, the opportunities for workers with permanent disabilities may have improved, leading to lower earnings losses and higher replacement rates.

This report summarizes our investigation of the relationship between earnings losses and economic conditions in California during the 1990s. Using a model developed for analyzing the impact of economic conditions (which is exposited in more detail in Reville and Schoeni, 2001), we were able to extrapolate from the model's estimates to provide predictions of long-term (five- and ten-year) wage losses and replacement rates for workers injured from 1991 to 1997. Including both self-insured and insured employers' claims in the predictions, these estimates provide the most current and comprehensive analysis of the adequacy of compensation in California to date.

We found significant improvements, on average, in outcomes for workers with PPD claims in California over the period 1991 through 1997. Specifically, we estimate that earnings losses (in 1997 dollars, before tax and before the payment of benefits) over the first five years after injury declined from $36,334 in 1991 to $33,572 in 1997 (with a low of $31,761 in 1994). We estimate that the decline in losses, combined with statutory benefit increases as a result of 1993 workers' compensation reforms, caused the fraction of these earnings losses that is replaced by workers' compensation indemnity benefits (the *replacement rate*) to increase from 0.52 in 1991 to 0.58 in 1997. The replacement rate over the ten years after injury increased from 0.43 to 0.46.

Most of the improvement occurs during the first three years of the study period, from 1991 through 1993, prior to the trough of the recession in California in late 1993. We found that while economic conditions at the time of injury have a limited effect on earnings losses of injured workers, this effect is largest for the least severely disabled claimants. Not only were the least-disabled claimants more likely to have better outcomes than more-disabled claimants after economic conditions improved, the overall decline in earnings losses and improvement in replacement rates for the least-disabled claimants were also larger than those for more-disabled claimants. In addition, the size of the decline in earnings losses for the least-disabled claimants was much greater than would have been predicted given the degree of improvement in economic conditions. In contrast, the most-disabled claimants experienced no change in their outcomes, and may even have lost some ground over the 1990s.

Using the replacement of two-thirds of pre-tax earnings as the standard for judging the adequacy of indemnity benefits (Berkowitz and Burton, 1987), the results of our examination suggest that despite improvement in the replacement rates over the 1990s, benefits are inadequate whether measured at five or ten years after injury. Our results also suggest that improvements in outcomes for less-disabled claimants may be more readily achieved with improvements in post-injury employment opportunities (which are more plentiful during better economic conditions). Improvements in outcomes for the most-disabled claimants are more likely to require PPD benefit increases.

CHAPTER 2

CHANGES IN ECONOMIC CONDITIONS AND PUBLIC POLICY OVER THE 1990s

A number of developments over the 1990s affected injured workers' wage losses and replacement rates in California. For instance, we expect that improved economic conditions in the state may have caused wage losses to decrease. In addition, changes in the workers' compensation program and changes in the laws regarding persons with disabilities may have affected both losses and replacement rates. We discuss these developments in this chapter.

ECONOMIC CONDITIONS

The estimates in Peterson et al. (1998), an earlier RAND report on the adequacy and equity of permanent disability benefits, were based on the experience of workers who were injured in 1991 and 1992. The five-year earnings losses that provided the focus of that report were based on workers injured in the first and second quarters of 1991. The statewide unemployment rate in the first quarter of 1991 was 7.8 percent. The unemployment rate rose to 10 percent by the third quarter of 1993 and then fell steadily, and was down to 5.1 percent by the third quarter of 2000. Therefore, workers injured in 1991 were injured in a deteriorating labor market.

For several reasons, wage losses may be greater for workers who are injured when the economy is weak. First, employers may be more reluctant to find modified work for an injured worker if employment at the firm is contracting. Therefore, the worker may be more likely to lose his or her job or, if modified work is available, that work may be lower paying. Second, other firms may be less likely to hire an injured worker when unemployment is high. This situation may imply longer periods of nonwork, or if employment is found at a new employer, the wages may be lower than they would be when the economy is strong.[1]

---

[1]Economic conditions may also affect the types of claims that are made. For instance, claims for less-severe injuries may be more likely with poor economic conditions. For this reason, we control for severity of injury in the analysis presented in Chapters 5 and 6. This will control for differences across disability ratings. However, it is also possible that *within* each disability rating, claims for less-severe injuries are more likely with poor economic conditions. With our data, we cannot distinguish this theory from the theory that emphasizes the impact of economic conditions on an employer's decision to offer employment to a partially disabled worker.

WORKERS' COMPENSATION REFORM

Changes in labor market conditions at the time of injury are not the only changes that may have affected workers' compensation claimants' outcomes over the study period. Workers' compensation reform legislation in 1993 deregulated workers' compensation insurance premiums, raised benefits for temporary disability and some PPD claimants, and included several provisions intended to reduce fraud. At least partly in response to these changes, but also following national trends, the number of injury claims and the number of PPD claims declined precipitously between 1991 and 1993. In 1991, there were 154,000 PPD claims in California. That number declined to 88,000 in 1993, and 82,000 in 1996. There were correspondingly large declines in workers' compensation losses and insurance premiums.[2]

Table 2.1 shows the changes in benefits for injured workers as a result of the 1993 legislation. These changes were phased in from 1994 to 1997, but the table shows only the pre-reform benefit levels (labeled "January 1991–June 1994" in the table) and the post–phase-in levels (labeled "July 1996–"). In California, temporary disability benefits are paid at two-thirds of the pre-tax pre-injury average weekly wage up to a maximum weekly amount. That maximum weekly amount increased with the 1993 legislation from $336 to $490. For many workers with PPDs (particularly those with lower-rated claims),[3] temporary disability benefits are a significant fraction of the total indemnity paid to them. Therefore, this increase in the maximum weekly amount would have increased total benefits paid on average per worker, for workers who are out of work after injury for the same or a greater amount of time.[4]

PPD benefits were also increased with the 1993 legislation. In California, total PPD benefits paid over the life of a claim increase more than proportionally with the disability rating for two reasons: (1) the number of weeks of benefits paid per disability rating point increases with the disability rating and (2) the weekly amount paid also increases. As shown in Table 2.1, in January 1991 through June 1994, workers with disability ratings below 25 received two-thirds of

---

[2]*CHSWC Annual Report, 1999–2000* (2000), citing the Workers' Compensation Insurance Rating Bureau.

[3]Permanent disability benefits are determined by a disability rating in California. Disability ratings range from 0 (no permanent disability) to 100 (total disability), and ratings of 1 through 99 denote permanent partial disability. The higher the rating, the more severe the injury is supposed to be, and the higher the number of weeks the worker is supposed to receive benefits (although, in practice, the future benefits are frequently converted into a lump sum and paid out when the claim is settled). The term "lower rated" is sometimes used interchangeably with the term "less severe" in this report.

[4]There is economics literature that shows that workers spend more time out of work when temporary disability maximum benefits are increased, in which case the increase in total benefits paid would exceed the statutory increase in maximum benefits (see, for instance, Meyer et al. [1995]). A CHSWC report on this subject, using information from the 1993 reform legislation, is being prepared by researchers at the University of California as of this writing.

Table 2.1

Maximum Weekly Payments for Temporary and Permanent Disability, Pre- and Post-1993 Legislation Levels

	January 1991–June 1994	July 1996–
	Temporary Disability Maximum Payment	
	$336	$490
Rating	Permanent Disability Maximum Payment	
1–14.75	$140	0
15–24.75	$140	$160
25–69.75	$148	$170
70–99.75	$148	$230

NOTE: Benefits are paid at two-thirds of the pre-injury pre-tax wage up to the maximum shown in this table.

their pre-injury wage up to a maximum of $140 per week. Workers with disability ratings of 25 or higher received a maximum benefit of $148. After July 1996, all workers with ratings of 15 or higher (approximately half of all PPD claimants) were receiving a greater weekly payment than they were before the 1993 legislation. The increase after July 1996 was particularly significant for claims with ratings of 70 or higher; workers with ratings at that level also received an increase in the life pension amount, although this group represents less than 5 percent of the claims.

Other changes in the 1993 legislation *reduced* benefits. These changes include caps on vocational rehabilitation, which may have reduced the payment of the vocational rehabilitation maintenance allowance (VRMA),[5] and restrictions on the compensability of psychiatric claims, which were frequently added to other PPD claims to increase the settlement amount.

Anecdotally, employers increased the use of return-to-work programs over the 1990s, which is partly in response to the high workers' compensation insurance premiums of the early 1990s. The increased use of return-to-work programs may lead to better long-term outcomes (lower wage losses) over time as more employers adopt these programs and if they effectively retain injured workers at or near their pre-injury wages. The increased use of these programs may also be related, in part, to the ability of employers after the 1993 legislation to avoid paying vocational rehabilitation if alternate and modified work is offered for one year from return to work. However, the long-term implications for workers receiving modified work instead of vocational rehabilitation over the year after injury are unknown.[6]

---

[5]VRMA is paid during vocational rehabilitation at a weekly maximum of $246, which had not changed over the 1990s.

[6]As of this writing, a CHSWC report is being prepared on this subject by researchers at the University of California.

AMERICANS WITH DISABILITIES ACT

Another significant change that occurred during the study period is the implementation of the Americans with Disabilities Act (ADA). Enforcement of the ADA, which passed in 1990, began in 1992. Awareness of the terms of the act increased over the 1990s. The equal pay and accommodation provisions of the ADA, if assumed by employers to apply to PPD claimants, may promote increased return to work and higher pay following a disabling injury.

Contrary to the expectations of advocates for the ADA, there is evidence that employment of the disabled declined during the 1990s. Explanations for the decline in employment have included employers' fear of possible litigation arising from the ADA and its impact on their hiring practices, in that employers may try to avoid the threat of litigation by not hiring disabled employees at all (Acemoglu and Angrist, 2001; Deleire, 2000), and the increasing availability of Social Security Disability Insurance (Bound and Waidmann, 2000).

CHAPTER 3

DEFINING WAGE LOSS AND REPLACEMENT RATES

We chose the replacement of earnings losses as our standard for measuring the adequacy of permanent partial disability benefits for three reasons: (1) It is the most straightforward way to measure the concept of work disability; (2) it is an extension of the standard for measuring temporary disability benefits; and (3) it is most likely the largest component of the economic losses experienced by disabled workers and therefore a reasonable target for compensation. In addition, there is literature (Berkowitz and Burton, 1987, for example) on adequacy of compensation that uses the replacement of earnings losses as the basis for this evaluation.

At the same time, this standard for measuring adequacy has several limitations. First, the California workers' compensation statute does not define PPD as "earnings loss" but rather as "the loss of ability to compete in the open labor market." Although earnings losses may be a closer proxy than the California rating schedule for the loss of ability to compete in the job market, earnings losses are not identified by the statute as an intended target for compensation. Second, and perhaps more important, earnings losses do not capture the full range of losses associated with a permanent disability that results from a workplace injury. For instance, earnings losses do not capture the loss of quality of life, inability to perform household or leisure activities, chronic pain or discomfort, or other potential consequences from serious injuries.

However, the workers' compensation system is typically described as a system whereby workers trade compensation for noneconomic losses for the right to have prompt compensation for economic losses and medical care on a no-fault basis. In addition, noneconomic losses are not readily measurable. Therefore, despite the limitations we just listed, we believe that earnings losses nevertheless are the best measure of the impact of a disabling workplace injury for the purpose of evaluating the adequacy of benefits.

Figure 3.1 presents the conceptual model used for our estimation of wage loss. The figure shows a hypothetical example of the earnings received by a worker with a PPD claim. The dashed line represents the earnings received by the worker if the injury had never occurred. Earnings are shown to be increasing over time, representing the higher pay associated with tenure and labor market experience. The solid line represents the earnings of the injured worker. In this example, the worker spends some time out of work starting at the point marked "Injury" on the horizontal

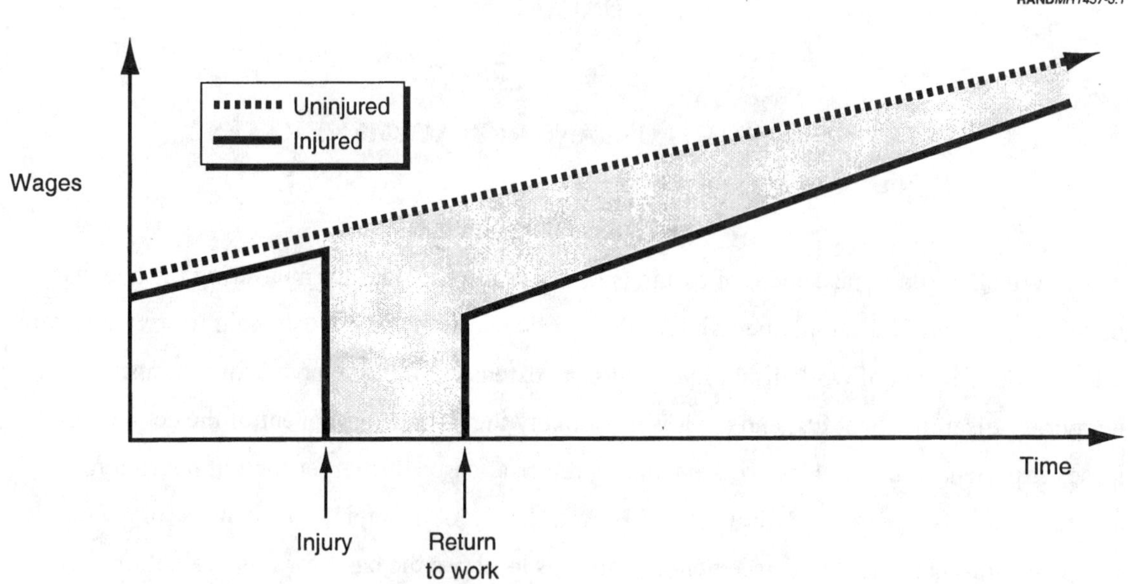

Figure 3.1—Hypothetical Earnings Loss of Injured Workers

axis. When the worker returns to work, he or she may return at his or her pre-injury wage; for this hypothetical example, we show the worker returning at a lower wage.

Figure 3.1 shows the worker's earnings increasing over time following his or her return to work. In the figure, the gap between the dashed line and the solid line narrows with time, representing *recovery* in earnings, but at the end of the period a gap nevertheless remains. The shaded area represents *wage loss*. The fraction of the shaded area that is replaced by workers' compensation benefits is the *replacement rate*.

One challenge in measuring wage loss is in determining the wages of the uninjured worker (represented by the dashed line in Figure 3.1) because we never observe what the injured worker would have earned in the absence of an injury. Our approach to this estimation problem is to use a matched comparison group. The comparison group consists of workers who worked at the same firm as the injured worker at the time of injury and who had the same earnings. For every injured worker, we have up to ten uninjured comparison workers from the same firm. Both the injured worker and the group of comparison workers are followed over the years after the injury. Wage loss is measured as the difference between the injured worker's earnings and the average of the earnings of the comparison workers for that injured worker.

For more information on the estimation of wage loss, see Peterson et al. (1998) and Reville et al. (2001). For discussion of the data on earnings and benefits paid to PPD claimants, see this report's appendix.

CHAPTER 4

WAGE LOSS AND REPLACEMENT RATES OVER THE 1990s

In this chapter, we explore trends in injured-worker outcomes over the 1990s. We demonstrate that injured workers' earnings losses declined over the decade, and explore the relationship between this decline in losses and the improved economy. We were not able to rule out that the improved outcomes for injured workers are related to the economy, and we also found that many alternative explanations for the trend in earnings losses are inconsistent with our data. The results presented in this chapter prompted our use of multivariate analytical methods, which we discuss in later chapters.

The data for this report are drawn from workers' compensation claims on injuries at both insured and self-insured private employers in California from 1991 through 1997. The data from both types of firms represent samples from the population of claims at those firms. For more information on the data, see the appendix.

Figure 4.1 shows the average earnings of injured workers at insured firms in California from 1991 to 1995 and the average earnings of our control group, or comparison workers, in each quarter relative to the quarter of injury.[1] (See Chapter 3 for a definition of the comparison group.) All claims in the sample from insured employers are included in the data used in creating Figure 4.1, and therefore the figure represents an average effect for workers with disabling injuries at insured firms from 1991 to 1995. Figure 4.1, which is similar to the figures in Peterson et al. (1998), demonstrates that the control workers are a close match to the injured workers. In the quarters leading up to injury, the earnings of the controls and injured workers are very similar; this is the case even several years prior to injury.[2]

The injured worker's quarterly earnings drop to 60 percent of the earnings of the control workers in the quarter after injury—the injured worker's earnings are down to $3,425, compared with $5,777 for the comparison workers. We estimate *earnings loss* as the difference between the injured worker's earnings and the comparison worker's earnings, or $2,352 in the quarter after

---

[1]Similar numbers are reported for self-insured employers in Reville et al. (2001).

[2]Note that earnings rise over the quarters leading up to the quarter of injury and then fall after injury. This is true for both the injured workers and their controls. This pattern is an artifact of the requirement that both the injured worker and the controls must be working in the quarter of injury. In surrounding quarters, workers are less likely to be working for one reason or another, and the farther away from the quarter of injury, the less likely they are to be working because of typical movements in and out of the labor force.

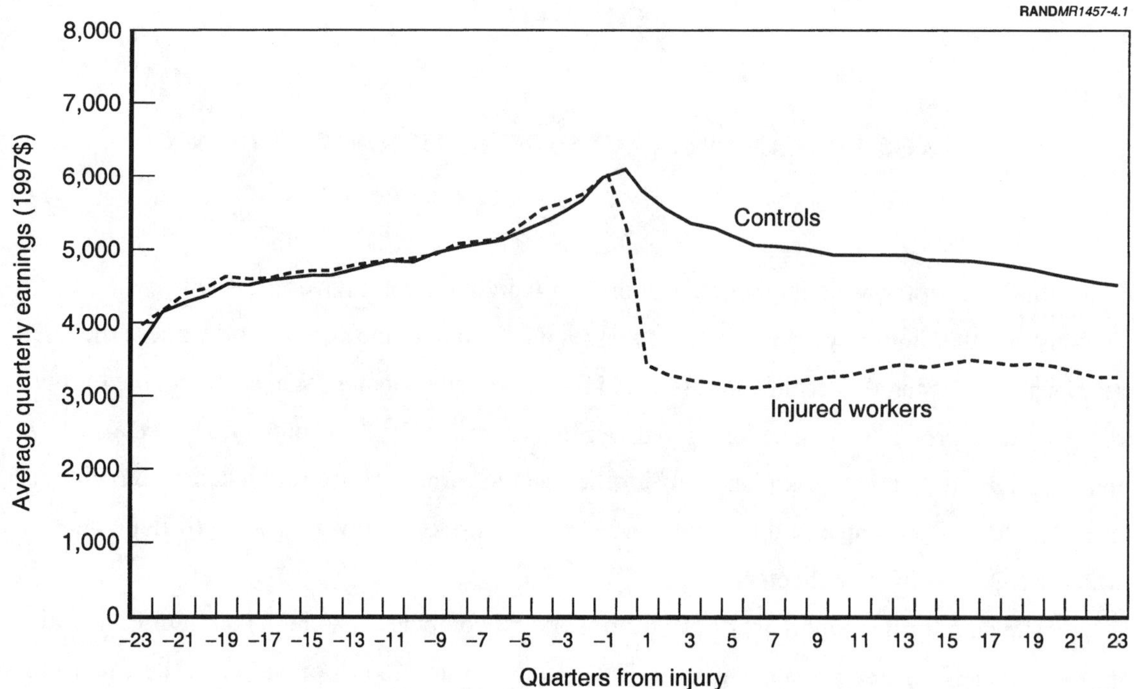

Figure 4.1—Average Earnings of Injured Workers and Control Workers by Quarters from Injury, PPD Claimants at Insured Firms in California, 1991–1995

injury. In the subsequent quarters, earnings begin to rebound relative to the control workers' earnings. However, the recovery is slow, and even five years after injury (20 quarters out), the injured worker is receiving only 73 percent of the earnings of control workers in that quarter. The difference between the injured worker's earnings and the comparison workers' earnings, or the quarterly earnings loss, is $1,257.

We estimate *total earnings losses* over the five years after injury by summing the quarterly earnings losses over the 20 quarters after injury, plus earnings losses during the quarter of injury. We then calculate proportional earnings losses by dividing the total earnings losses by the total amount that the comparison workers make over that time period.

Figure 4.2 demonstrates that the five-year proportional earnings loss in our insured firm data declined between 1991 and 1993, whereas almost no change is observed in the earnings loss in our self-insured-firm data. Workers injured in the first quarter of 1991 at insured firms experienced proportional earnings losses of roughly 42 percent, whereas workers injured in the fourth quarter of 1993 at insured firms had proportional earnings losses of about 30 percent. Workers at self-insured firms experienced proportional wage losses between 21 percent and 25 percent throughout the period.

The dashed lines in Figure 4.2 denote 95-percent confidence bounds for proportional wage loss. Those dashed lines imply that over the entire period, the proportional earnings loss for

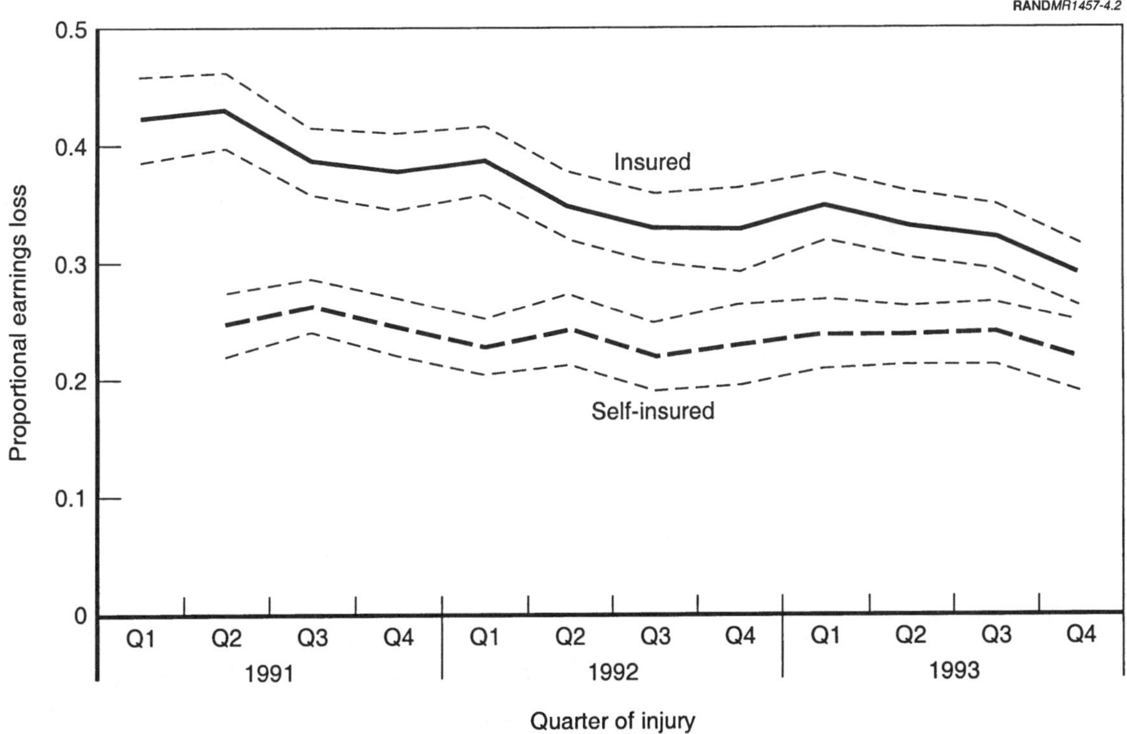

Figure 4.2—Five-Year Proportional Earnings Loss by Quarter of Injury, PPD Claimants at Insured and Self-Insured Firms in California, 1991–1993

workers injured at insured firms is higher than that for workers at self-insured firms, as discussed in Reville et al. (2001). More to the point, however, the confidence interval also indicates that the decline in proportional wage loss at insured firms is statistically significant.[3]

Figure 4.3 examines replacement rates over five years after an injury occurs (which we refer to as *five-year replacement rates*) by quarter of injury for claimants at insured and self-insured firms. For example, the five-year replacement rate for a worker injured at an insured firm in the third quarter of 1991 is slightly more than 50 percent. For simplicity's sake, the 95-percent confidence interval is reported for insured firms only. Replacement rates at insured and self-insured firms are similar over the entire study period. Associated with the decline in proportional wage loss for workers injured at insured firms is a statistically significant increase in the replacement rate for workers at insured firms.

Figure 4.4 includes workers injured more recently, in 1994 and 1995, as well as workers injured from 1991 to 1993. We examined earnings losses for just three years following injury because the earnings data are available only through the fourth quarter of 1998. As was shown in

[3]The standard errors for construction of the confidence interval are calculated using a "bootstrap" method. See Efron and Tibshirani (1993) for more information on this method.

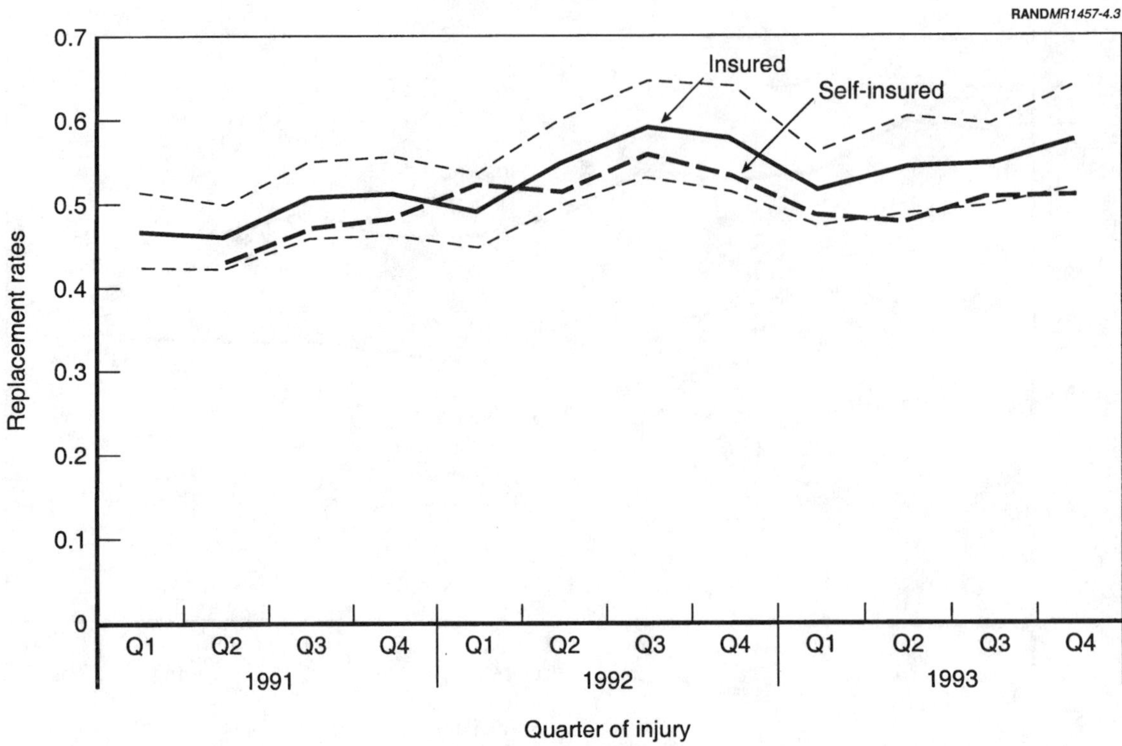

Figure 4.3—Five-Year Replacement Rates by Quarter of Injury, PPD Claimants at Insured and Self-Insured Firms in California, 1991–1993

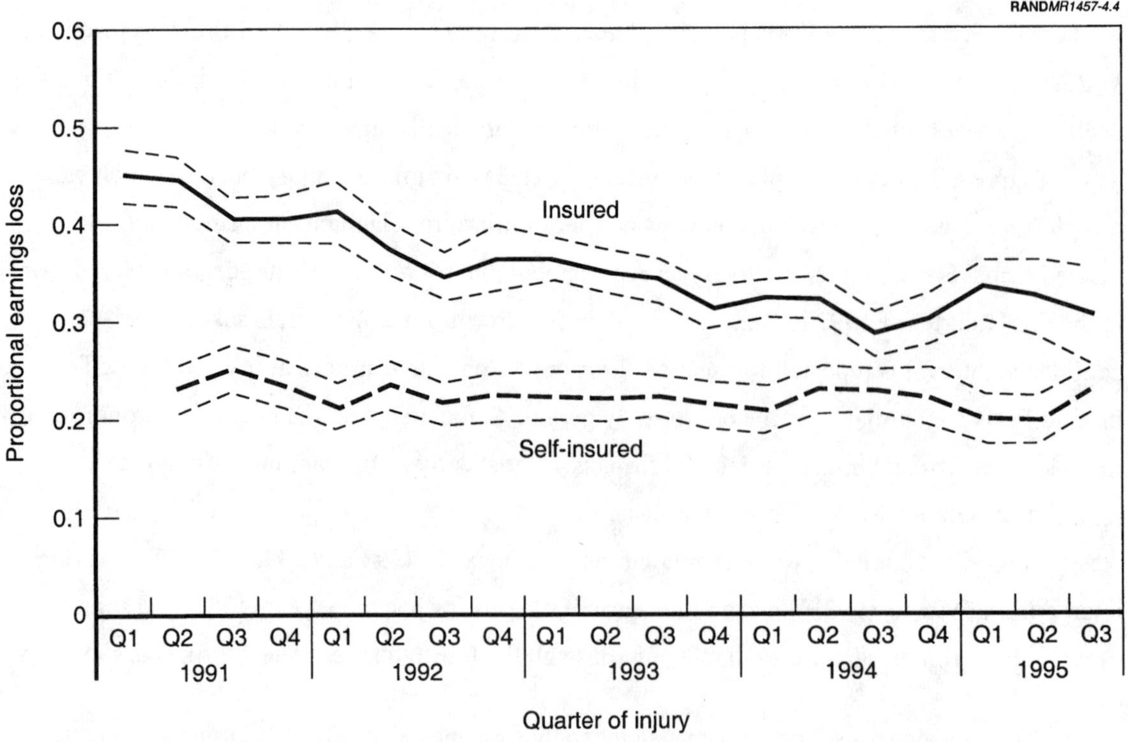

Figure 4.4—Three-Year Proportional Earnings Loss by Quarter of Injury, PPD Claimants at Insured and Self-Insured Firms in California, 1991–1995

Figure 4.2, proportional earnings loss as reflected in our insured firm data fell between the first quarter of 1991 and the fourth quarter of 1993.

However, despite the fact that the labor market expanded after 1993, earnings losses did not continue to fall. In fact, the proportional earnings loss was identical for workers injured in the fourth quarter of 1995 (the most recent estimate) and the second quarter of 1993.

Figure 4.4 also shows the trend in proportional earnings losses for workers as reflected in our private-firm self-insured employer data. As shown in Figure 4.4, workers at self-insured firms experienced no change in proportional earnings losses throughout the entire 1991 to 1995 period. As a result, the rest of our analyses on trends and the impact of economic conditions will focus on the insured population. However, in Chapter 6, where we report statewide estimates for 1991 to 1997, self-insured claimants are included in the data.

IMPROVEMENTS ARE NOT EXPLAINED BY CHANGES IN THE COMPOSITION OF CLAIMS

Policymakers are likely to be interested in the reasons for the decline in earnings losses for workers who were injured at insured firms in 1991 to 1995. They would want to be able to assess whether the decline is likely to have continued during the second half of the 1990s. For instance, if economic conditions explain the improvement in outcomes, it is likely that earnings losses continued to decline given that economic conditions continued to improve after 1995. In this section, we explore some potential explanations for this trend using graphics and descriptive data, before turning to the analyses in Chapter 5, where we use a statistical model.

One potential explanation for the decline in earnings losses is that the composition of claims changed. For example, Peterson et al. (1998) demonstrated that proportional earnings losses were larger for more-severe injuries. Therefore, if workers injured more recently are experiencing less-severe injuries, then such a change in composition could account for the improvement in outcomes. Table 4.1 reports the composition of our sample of workers who were injured in 1991, 1993, and 1995. The workers are categorized by several factors: severity of injury (according to their average disability rating), pre-injury earnings, firm size, and claims in three Southern California counties as a fraction of all claims in the state. The table also reports the composition of the sample according to the Workers' Compensation Insurance Rating Bureau (WCIRB)[4] report level at which the claim closed (claim-closing levels are discussed later in this section).

---

[4]The WCIRB is a private entity responsible for publishing and proposing workers' compensation insurance premium rates.

Table 4.1

Change in the Composition of Injured Workers

	Injured in 1991	Injured in 1993	Injured in 1995
Average disability rating	19.4	20.5	20.3
Pre-injury quarterly earnings	$6,018	$6,006	$6,046
Firm size (by number of employees)			
Mean	1,877	1,076	781
25th percentile	50	42	39
Median	135	121	116
75th percentile	416	403	345
Los Angeles/Orange/San Bernardino Counties (% of all claimants)	0.434	0.288	0.301
Report level at claim closing			
Early-closing claim	0.006	0.119	0.148
Medium-closing claim	0.041	0.231	0.247
Late-closing claim	0.953	0.650	0.605

Severity of Injury

Figure 4.5 demonstrates earnings losses for five equally sized groups of workers categorized by severity of injury, as measured by their disability ratings. Not surprisingly, workers with the most-severe injuries suffer the largest earnings losses—60- to 70-percent proportional earnings losses for the most severely injured (those with disability ratings from 32 to 99) versus 10- to 30-percent losses for the least severely injured (those with ratings from 0 to 5). Most important, proportional earnings loss declined between the first quarter of 1991 and the fourth quarter of 1993 for all severity levels. Moreover, there was little or no improvement between the fourth quarter of 1993 and the fourth quarter of 1995 within any severity level.

At the same time, there was a modest shift in the composition of injuries, with injuries in 1995 being slightly *more* severe than injuries in 1991 (see Table 4.1). Because more-severely injured workers have larger earnings losses, the increase in severity between 1991 and 1995 works in the opposite direction of the observed overall change in earnings losses. Therefore, the aggregate decline in earnings losses cannot be explained by changes in the severity of claims.

The relative size of the improvement in outcomes in terms of earnings losses among severity-of-injury groups is noteworthy. Although Figure 4.5 does not control for other changes that may have occurred simultaneously, it suggests that workers with the least severe injuries experienced the largest improvements, whereas workers with the most severe injuries experienced only a small improvement. Proportional earnings losses among the least severely injured PPD claimants declined from almost 30 percent in 1991 to approximately 10 percent by 1995. In

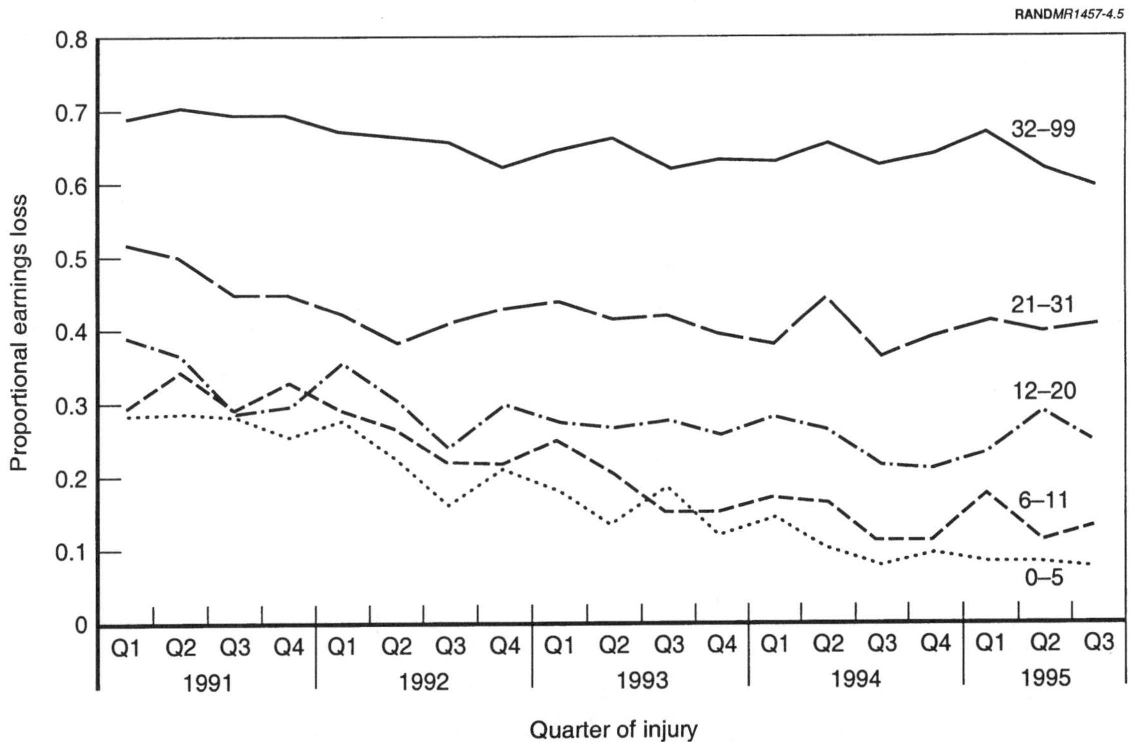

Figure 4.5—Three-Year Proportional Earnings Loss by Quarter of Injury and Severity (Disability Rating), PPD Claimants at Insured Firms in California, 1991–1995

contrast, the proportional earning losses among the most severely injured PPD claimants declined from 70 percent to approximately 60 percent. In Chapter 6, our statewide estimates reinforce this difference across severity groups, demonstrating almost no change for the most severely injured PPD claimants and large improvements for the least severely injured PPD claimants.

Firm Size

Reville et al. (2001) and Reville and Schoeni (2001) showed that larger firm size leads to lower proportional wage losses. If firm size increased between 1991 and 1995, this may have partly explained the decreases in proportional earnings losses over that same period. In Figure 4.6, we divide workers into four groups based on the size (by number of employees) of their at-injury employer. We find that all four groups experienced declines in their proportional earnings loss between 1991 and 1993. The proportional earnings loss for workers injured at both the smallest and largest firms fell by roughly ten percentage points. Moreover, the declines continue to be concentrated within the 1991 to 1993 period, with little change occurring after 1993.

The composition of the sample with regard to the size of the firms where the workers were injured changed substantially from 1991 to 1995. The median firm size fell from 135 for workers injured in 1991 to 116 for workers injured in 1995. Moreover, this drop in firm size

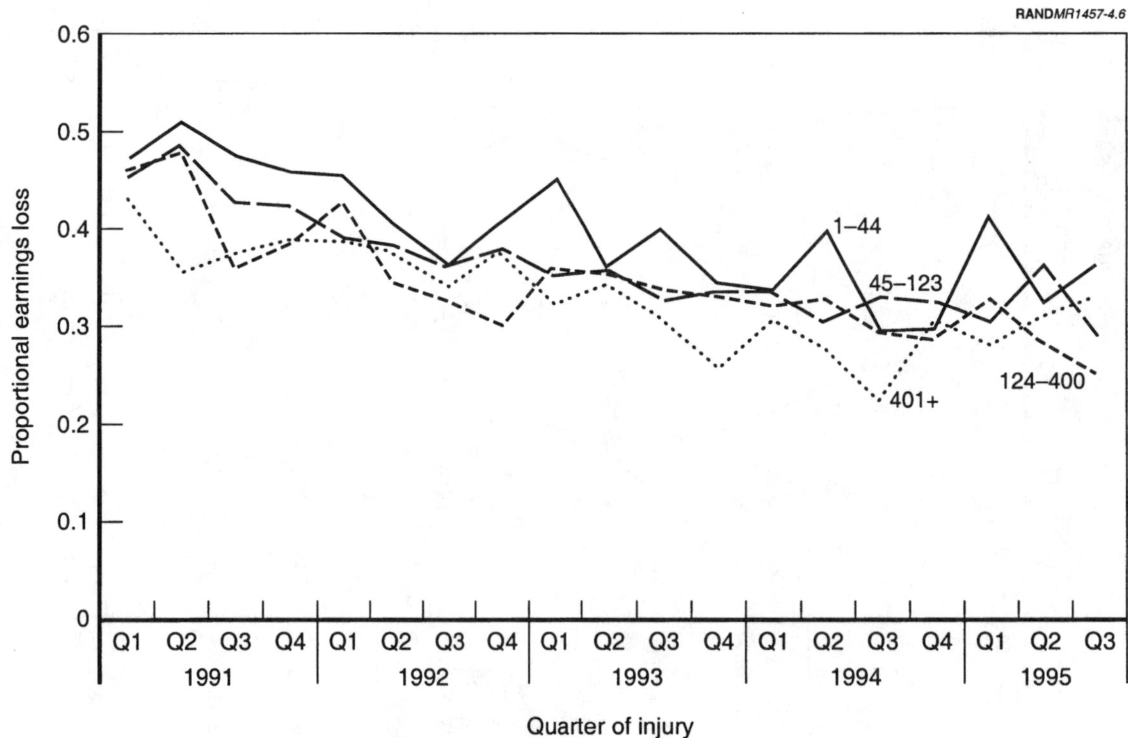

Figure 4.6—Three-Year Proportional Earnings Loss by Quarter of Injury and Firm Size, PPD Claimants at Insured Firms in California, 1991–1995

appears throughout the firm-size distribution (see Table 4.1). Because workers injured at smaller firms experience larger losses, a trend toward smaller-sized firms would imply larger losses over time in California, which is contrary to what we observed. Therefore, changes in firm size do not explain the decline in wage loss.

County of Employment

Figure 4.7 displays proportional earnings losses by quarter of injury for Los Angeles County and the San Francisco County group.[5] Although San Francisco County experienced improvements (a decline in proportional earnings losses) over the study period, most of the change occurred in Los Angeles County where proportional earnings losses declined from about 47 percent in 1991 to 32 percent in 1995. Among the other county groups (not shown), the declines were similar to those in San Francisco, or, in some cases, there were no improvements. The only exceptions were the other Los Angeles–basin counties (Orange, Riverside, and San

[5]Some California counties were grouped together because the sample sizes were not large enough in many counties to accurately estimate earnings loss. The groupings were based on geography and similarity in patterns of earnings loss. The 13 individual counties and county groups are listed in the appendix.

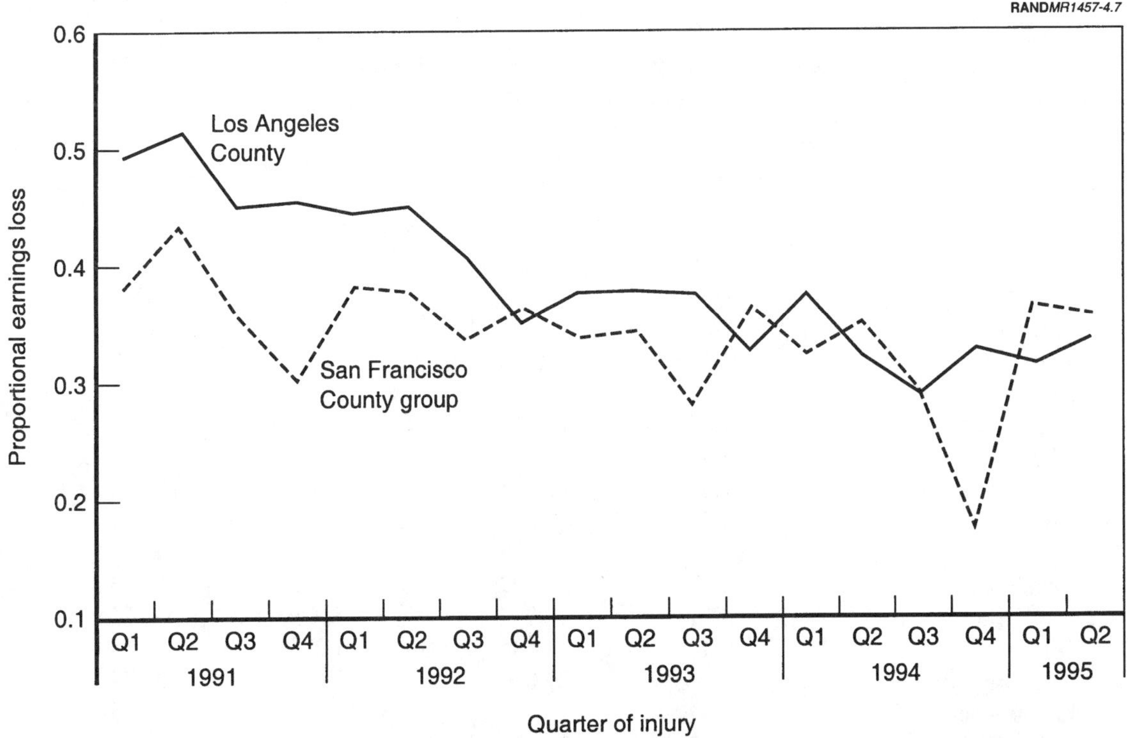

Figure 4.7—Three-Year Proportional Earnings Loss by Quarter and County of Injury, PPD Claimants at Insured Firms in California, 1991–1995

Bernardino), which experienced nearly the identical magnitude of improvement as Los Angeles County.

Table 4.2 demonstrates that the share of claims in the state that were made in Los Angeles, Orange, or San Bernardino Counties declined from 43 percent in 1991 to 30 percent in 1995. While the entire state experienced declines in the number of claims, the decline was largest in the Los Angeles basin, precisely the region that was observed with the largest earnings losses in 1991. However, this change in the claims composition cannot explain the statewide decline in earnings loss. If the distribution of claims across the state had remained as it was in 1991 (for example, Los Angeles County having 33.5 percent of the claims), but the change in earnings losses *within* counties had not occurred as shown in Figure 4.7, the statewide three-year earnings loss would have declined by only $190 (from $27,798 to $27,608). Therefore, the change in the distribution of claims across counties can account for just 5 percent of the $3,923 decline (from $27,798 to $23,875, reported in the bottom row of Table 4.2) between 1991 and 1995.

Claim-Closing Level

A limitation in the WCIRB data provided to RAND was that the individual identifiers of the claimants were not available until the WCIRB revised its reporting requirements beginning in

Table 4.2

Three-Year Cumulative Earnings Loss by County or County Group for Workers Injured in 1991 and 1995

	Injured in 1991		Injured in 1995	
County or County Group	Proportion of Claims (%)	Three-Year Cumulative Earnings Loss ($)	Proportion of Claims (%)	Three-Year Cumulative Earnings Loss ($)
Sacramento	2.6	29,995	3.6	31,573
North	1.3	25,618	1.9	21,288
San Francisco	5.1	27,651	8.4	28,157
San Joaquin	2.0	23,888	2.1	21,141
Alameda	2.4	32,375	4.0	26,724
Santa Clara	2.6	31,444	3.4	19,133
Riverside	2.7	27,687	3.4	22,140
Fresno	4.3	20,889	5.2	24,572
Central Coast	2.4	24,120	3.5	19,633
San Diego	3.7	18,037	6.0	23,166
Orange	7.4	27,484	6.9	22,160
San Bernardino	2.4	29,090	2.4	20,978
Los Angeles	33.5	27,703	20.7	22,228
Missing/other	27.5	30,175	28.4	24,872
Statewide	100.0	27,798	100.0	23,875

1993. These identifiers were used to link the data to earnings data, and when those data were unavailable, the claim could not be used in the analysis. Insurers report annually to the WCIRB on the status of all open PPD claims, and if claims are still open by the insurers' 1993 report to the WCIRB, Social Security numbers were usually also reported. This leads to a compositional difference across years. In particular, there are relatively few early-closing claims (closed within 18 months from the time the insurance policy is initiated or renewed) in 1991 and 1992. As was shown in Table 4.1, less than 1 percent of claims in our sample in 1991 were early-closing, more than 95 percent were late-closing (closed at least 30 months after initiation or renewal), and 4 percent were medium-closing (closed between 18 and 30 months after initiation or renewal). By 1993, just 65 percent of claims were late-closing, whereas 12 percent were early-closing and 23 percent were medium-closing.

We found that workers with late-closing claims tend to have higher earnings losses. Figure 4.8 shows the earnings losses by quarter of injury and level of claim, with only those quarters having more than 50 injuries being included. It is clear from the figure that when early-closing claims are averaged in for the later quarters, the overall average falls. However, even among late-closing claims, which account for the vast majority of claims in any year, proportional earnings

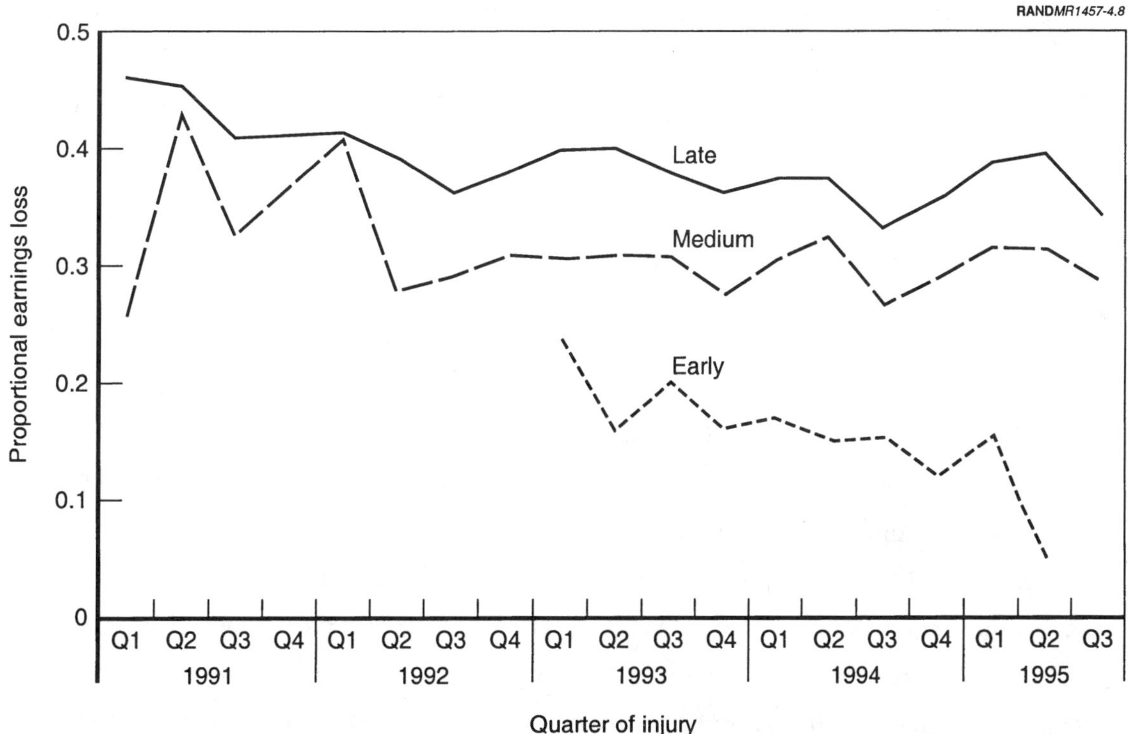

Figure 4.8—Three-Year Proportional Earnings Loss by Quarter of Injury and Claim-Closing Level, PPD Claimants at Insured Firms, 1991–1995

losses declined between 1991 and 1993. For further discussion of this aspect of the data, see Peterson et al. (1998).

In the statistical analysis we present in Chapter 5, we include controls for the "level" of the claim, which is defined as early-, medium-, or late-closing. As suggested by the trend shown in Figure 4.8, we would find that the size of the decline in earnings losses is reduced after controlling for this compositional change (in particular, our estimates for 1991 without this correction are biased upward), but the results with regard to changes over the 1990s are not substantially altered.

In sum, declines in earnings loss have been widespread. Regardless of severity, firm size, county of employment, or report level, proportional losses declined between the beginning of 1991 and the end of 1993. Further broad-based gains were not achieved after 1993. Moreover, the composition of the sample with respect to industry, firm size, severity, and county of employment has not changed enough over this period to account for more than a small fraction of the improvements in worker outcomes.

ECONOMIC CONDITIONS EXPLAIN ONLY SOME OF THE IMPROVEMENTS

Before turning to the statistical model estimates in the next chapter, we examine the evidence with regard to the importance of economic conditions by using two kinds of descriptive data. First, for the state as a whole, we determined whether the time pattern of earnings loss rises and falls with economic conditions—that is, we examined "time series evidence." Second, we determined whether counties with better economic conditions tend to experience lower earnings losses—that is, we examined "cross-county evidence."

Time-Series Evidence

Figure 4.9 plots three-year proportional earnings loss by quarter of injury. Also on the chart is the unemployment rate and employment growth rate[6] for the state of California in each quarter from 1991 through 2000. This chart shows that when proportional earnings losses were falling between 1991 and 1993, the unemployment rate was actually rising. And when the unemployment rate finally began to fall in 1994, earnings losses remained steady. The employment growth rate tracks proportional earnings losses more closely, rising in the 1991 to 1992 period when proportional earnings losses experienced their largest improvement. And both employment growth and proportional earnings losses were fairly flat between 1993 and 1995. However, the relationship is not perfect. Despite the fact that employment growth was unchanged between the fourth quarter of 1992 and the fourth quarter of 1993, earnings losses declined from 37 percent to 32 percent. Nonetheless, the simple correlation between the employment growth rate and proportional wage loss is 0.86, which suggests that the two may be closely related.

Cross-County Evidence

Table 4.3 ranks the 13 counties and county groups by proportional earnings loss for workers injured in 1991. Also shown are the unemployment rate and the employment growth rate in 1991. This table demonstrates that, across counties, the simple association between labor market conditions and proportional earnings loss is weak. Counties or county groups with low unemployment rates or high employment growth rates do not necessarily have low proportional earnings loss. In fact, the correlation in employment growth and county earnings loss is *positive* 0.18.

It is possible that there are long-term differences across counties in the level of proportional wage loss that is driven by the industrial mix of employers, average skill level of employees, or other factors in a county that may be unrelated to the employment growth rate.

---

[6]Employment growth rate is calculated as the proportional increase in employment in one quarter over the previous quarter's employment.

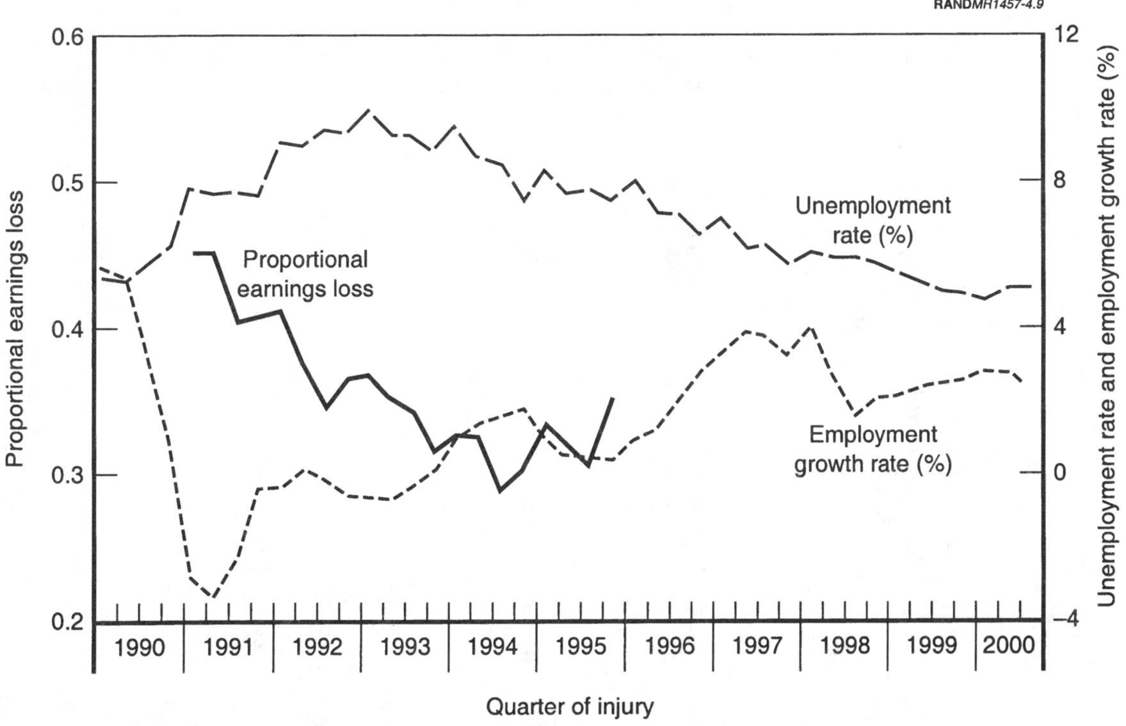

Figure 4.9—Three-Year Proportional Earnings Loss by Quarter of Injury and Economic Conditions in California, PPD Claimants at Insured Firms

However, improvements in the labor market over time within a county may lead to improvements in wage loss for workers in that county. These kinds of differences across counties may obscure the impact of improved economic conditions on earnings loss, especially when the data are as reported in Table 4.3. To investigate this possibility, we rank counties by the *change* in three-year proportional earnings loss between 1991 and 1995 (see Table 4.4). By examining changes in these outcomes, we find that earnings losses are more negatively related to the employment growth rate than would be implied by the simple association across counties that is shown in Table 4.3. In particular, the largest decline in earnings losses occurred in Santa Clara County, which also experienced the largest increase in quarterly employment growth. However, a similarly large improvement in economic conditions in San Diego County is associated with an increase in proportional earnings loss. The simple correlation is –0.49.

As with the time-series evidence described earlier, the changes within counties suggest that economic conditions are an important determinant of long-term outcomes for injured workers. This suggests that a careful analysis of the data, examining the impact of economic conditions while controlling for changes in other factors, is warranted. We turn to this analysis in the next chapter.

Table 4.3

Rank of Counties and County Groups by Proportional Earnings Loss for Workers Injured in 1991

County or County Group	Proportional Earnings Loss (%)	Unemployment Rate (%)	Average Quarterly Employment Growth Rate (%)
San Diego	30.8	6.3	–0.381
Santa Clara	35.2	5.7	–0.400
San Francisco	37.0	5.3	0.009
Fresno	38.7	13.3	0.457
Alameda	38.9	5.3	–0.391
San Joaquin	39.3	13.3	–0.073
North	41.5	11.0	0.144
Central Coast	43.8	6.8	–0.115
Sacramento	45.2	6.7	0.147
Orange	45.4	5.3	–0.669
Los Angeles	48.0	8.2	0.047
Riverside	49.3	11.0	0.068
San Bernardino	50.1	8.0	–0.185

Table 4.4

Rank of Counties and County Groups by Change in Proportional Earnings Loss and Change in Labor Market Indicators Between 1991 and 1995

County or County Group	Proportional Earnings Loss, 1995 (%)	Change in Proportional Earnings Loss (%)	Change in Average Quarterly Employment Growth (%)
San Diego	34.1	–3.3	–0.60
Fresno	41.6	–2.9	0.57
North	39.8	1.7	0.17
Sacramento	43.4	1.8	–0.12
San Francisco	33.7	3.3	0.02
San Joaquin	33.3	6.0	0.15
Alameda	29.6	9.3	–0.41
Central Coast	33.8	10.0	0.24
Riverside	37.1	12.2	–0.25
San Bernardino	34.6	15.5	–0.29
Los Angeles	32.1	15.8	–0.06
Orange	29.4	16.0	–0.67
Santa Clara	19.1	16.1	–1.26

CHAPTER 5

ACCOUNTING FOR CONFOUNDING FACTORS BY USING A STATISTICAL MODEL

In this chapter, we develop and estimate a statistical model of the relationship between economic conditions and trends in earnings losses from a permanently disabling injury. The descriptive relationship between earnings losses and economic conditions over time and across counties, as presented in Chapter 4, is unsatisfactory for both research and policy reasons. From a research standpoint, the results are inconclusive because in order to isolate the impact of economic conditions, we need to account for factors other than economic ones that may covary with those conditions. From a policy perspective, the results are unsatisfactory because estimation of long-term earnings losses requires observing an individual several years after injury and, inevitably, the estimates will be for injuries that are relatively old. Policymakers would rightfully question the relevance of such estimates to current policy questions. It is preferable to develop a framework that would permit prediction of outcomes for recently injured workers in current economic conditions.

For Reville and Schoeni (2001), a multivariate statistical model was developed that describes the pattern of earnings loss. This model allows us to statistically hold constant other factors that may confound estimates of the relationship between economic conditions and injured workers' earnings losses. The results of the analyses based on this multivariate statistical model will be discussed in this chapter. In addition, the modeling approach allows us to predict wage losses in two ways. First, using information about the employer's industry, the injured worker's pre-injury earnings, the severity of the injury, and economic conditions at the time of injury, as well as the pattern of earnings over the years after injury, we are able to estimate five- and ten-year earnings losses for all injury years 1991 to 1995 with wage data that for 1994 and 1995 cover less than five years. Second, using information on the relationship among key factors (economic conditions at the time of injury, pre-injury earnings, and severity of the injury) between 1991 and 1995, and using severity and wage information from more-recent claims data and data on economic conditions in California, we estimate the losses of workers injured more recently, specifically in 1996 and 1997. The results from these analyses are described in Chapter 6.

THE MODELING APPROACH

The key statistical technique we employ is a multivariate regression model that relates earnings losses to a variety of characteristics of the injured worker. The model allows us to examine these factors simultaneously so that one can look at the effects of severity of an injury, for example, while holding constant the industry in which the worker was employed. The variable under consideration (that is, the *dependent variable*) is the quarterly earnings loss for each worker. The factors that the model relates to earnings loss (that is, the *explanatory variables*) include severity of injury, wages prior to injury, industry, firm size of employer at the time of injury, and economic conditions in the county in which the worker was employed. We model the pattern of earnings losses using three variables: the *dip,* the *drop,* and the *recovery.* We then allow this pattern of earnings losses—the dip, drop, and recovery—to vary by the various characteristics (such as severity of injury) of the injured worker.

The basic approach can be explained by looking at Figure 4.1 in Chapter 4. In that figure, there is a small decline in earnings in the quarter of injury (Quarter 0). That decline is the dip. In the following quarter, the quarter after injury, earnings loss is at its greatest. That earnings loss is the drop. In subsequent quarters, we observe continued earnings loss, but the loss becomes smaller in each quarter. Therefore, the third variable is the recovery, or the average quarterly decline in the loss experienced at the drop.

The solid line in Figure 5.1 labeled "Actual quarterly earnings loss" is based on the exact same information that was used for Figure 4.1, except that it is shown in terms of *earnings loss* instead of earnings. The difference in earnings between injured workers and their comparison workers is calculated for every injured worker, and the average difference across all injured workers is displayed in the figure. This set of estimates is not based on the multivariate model, but is based on the simple difference between the earnings of injured workers and the earnings of their comparison coworkers who had similar earnings prior to injury.

Figure 5.1 also displays the estimates of dip, drop, and recovery (shown by the dashed line) that were estimated in the regression model before the competing factors—severity of injury, industry, and the rest—were included. (See Reville and Schoeni [2001] for details.) The average dip in earnings is $884, which is followed by an average drop of $2,249 in the following quarter. In every subsequent quarter, the drop declines by $48.50. The estimates from the regression model are almost identical to the estimates based on the simple comparison between the earnings of the injured workers and their comparison coworkers in each quarter. Therefore, the statistical model provides a good fit to the data, and therefore can be a useful tool for prediction.

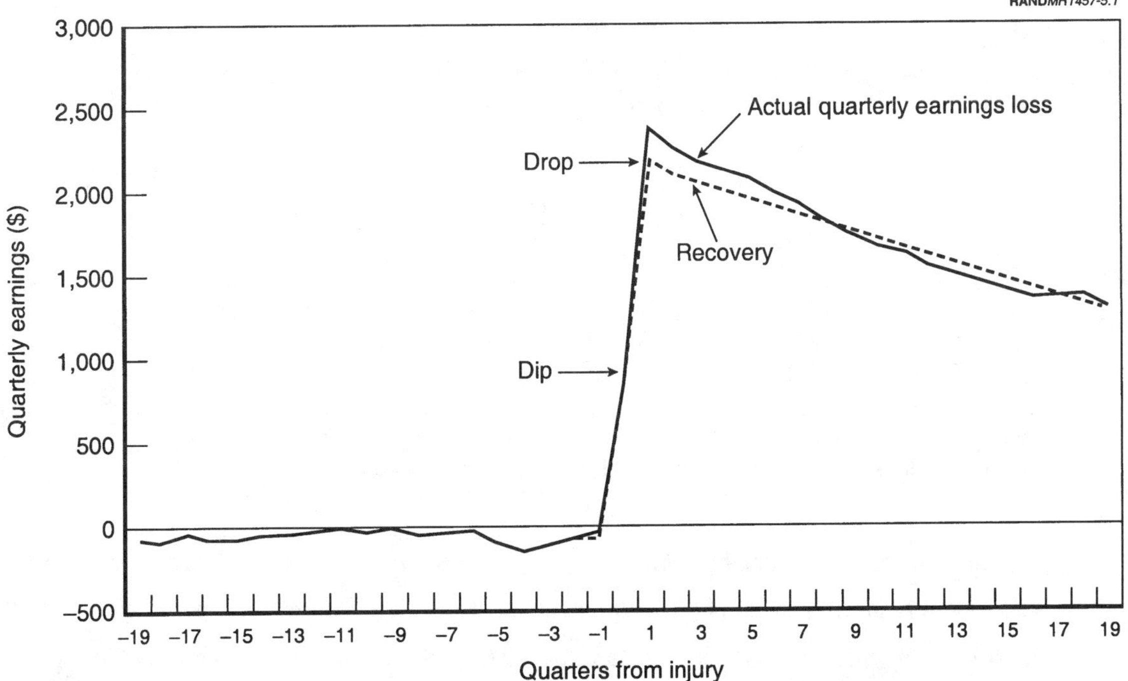

Figure 5.1—Earnings Loss Based on Dip, Drop, and Recovery of Earnings Compared with Actual Quarterly Earnings Loss, PPD Claimants at Insured Firms in California, 1991–1995

Before describing the results that include the full set of confounding factors, it is useful to consider the intermediate step in which we simply include one explanatory factor in the multivariate regression model, that factor being severity of injury. Table 5.1 reports the estimates of dip, drop, and recovery of earnings for the overall sample and for five injury severity groups that are defined by disability rating.[1] The table also shows estimates of quarterly earnings losses at two and four years following injury that use the dip, drop, and recovery parameter estimates. For example, the quarterly loss two years (eight quarters) after injury is equivalent to the drop plus seven times the recovery because there are seven quarters of recovery in the initial drop in the quarter after injury. This implies that, eight quarters after injury, the average PPD claimant will lose $1,910. Between two and four years after injury, claimants will continue to experience losses attenuated by continuing recovery until, by four years after injury, the quarterly losses are $1,522.

Table 5.1 also shows that the least-severely injured workers, those with disability ratings of 1 to 5, experience a drop ($1,364) that is about one-third the size of the drop ($3,830) experienced by the most-severely injured workers, those with disability ratings above 30. In each

[1]As noted previously, these estimates and all estimates drawn from Reville and Schoeni (2001) use data from insured firms only.

Table 5.1

Dip, Drop, and Recovery Estimates of Earnings: Whole Sample and by Injury Severity Group, 1991–1995

	Dip ($)	Drop ($)	Recovery ($)	Quarterly Earnings Loss ($) at 2 Years	4 Years
All claims	884	2,249	–48.5	1,910	1,522
Rating 1–5	715	1,364	–32.5	1,136	876
Rating 6–10	740	1,423	–34.5	1,181	905
Rating 11–19	831	1,852	–45.6	1,533	1,168
Rating 20–30	954	2,660	–59.1	2,246	1,773
Rating 31–99	1,164	3,830	–64.7	3,377	2,859

NOTE: Estimates are based on regressions without controlling for other factors.

subsequent quarter, the recovery of the most-severely injured workers is larger than the recovery of the least-severely injured workers ($64.70 for the most-severely injured, compared with $32.50 for the least-severely injured), but given the size of the overall impact (as measured by the drop), the most-severely injured workers do not catch up to the least-severely injured ones. The latter group experiences quarterly losses of $1,136 two years after injury and quarterly losses of $876 four years after injury. In contrast, the most-severely injured workers have quarterly losses of $3,377 two years after injury and losses of $2,859 four years after injury.

Given this approach of summarizing the impact of the injury using the three variables (dip, drop, and recovery), it is possible to estimate the impact of injury for a large number of subgroups simultaneously, and to hold constant some factors while varying others. Specifically, we use this approach to examine the impact of economic conditions on the path of earnings loss after injury, holding constant factors other than economic ones that affect injury and that may have been changing at the same time. In addition to economic conditions at the time of injury, we controlled for six factors: severity of injury, pre-injury earnings, firm size, industry, time trend, and level of closing of the claim.

RESULTS

Table 5.2 summarizes the estimates for the model that include all of the confounding variables (and not just severity, as in Table 5.1), while focusing on the impact of local economic conditions. We represent local economic conditions as those conditions that existed in the county of employment at the time of injury. We estimated models measuring local economic conditions by using the county unemployment rate and the county employment growth rate. There was no

Table 5.2

Change in Dip, Drop, and Recovery of Earnings with Improved Economic Conditions: Whole Sample and by Injury Severity Group

	Dip (%)	Drop (%)	Recovery (%)
All claims	–2.67	–21.37	0.74
Rating 1–5	–27.70	–43.92	1.70
Rating 6–10	11.68	20.59	–0.36
Rating 11–19	–13.40	–20.98	2.16
Rating 20–30	–2.06	–20.77	–0.19
Rating 31–99	11.35	–27.99	–0.05

NOTE: This table shows the impact of a one-percentage-point increase in county employment growth. Estimates are based on regressions controlling for industry, pre-injury wage, firm size, and late-closing claims. See Reville and Schoeni (2001), Table 4.1 for all claims and Table 4.3 for estimates by Rating Group.

association between earnings losses and the unemployment rate; therefore, the unemployment rate is excluded from the models presented here.[2]

Estimates from two different models are reported in Table 5.2. First, in the row labeled "All claims," estimates of the impact of economic conditions for all PPD claimants from first quarter 1991 through fourth quarter 1995 are reported. In the rows labeled with the disability ratings, the impact of economic conditions is allowed to differ depending on the severity of the claim.

Focusing first on the "All claims" estimates, we find that the impact of local economic conditions is not large. To interpret the estimates, it helps to know that the statewide quarterly employment growth rate ranged from a low of –0.03 in the second quarter of 1991 to a high of 0.04 in the first quarter of 1998: a range of 0.07 from the trough to the peak. But these are the extremes. The ninetieth to the tenth percentile of employment growth rate across counties from 1991 to 1995 in California is a range of 0.03.

Table 5.2 reports the change in dip, drop, and recovery of earnings associated with an increase of 0.01 in employment growth. A 0.03 employment growth increase will decrease the dip by only three times $2.67 or approximately $8 (compared with an average level of the dip of $884, as shown in Table 5.1), and will decrease the drop by only three times $21.37 or approximately $64 (compared with an average drop of $2,249, as shown in Table 5.1). In

[2]We also explored whether the current economic conditions in the time *after* injury (rather than the economic conditions at the time *of* injury) have an effect, and found no evidence for this kind of effect and also no evidence that controlling for this effect changed our estimates of time-of-injury economic-condition effects. Furthermore, we explored whether the economic conditions at the end of temporary disability were more likely to affect wage loss. Those conditions also had no effect. The results reported in Table 5.2 are the most supportive of the argument that economic conditions matter.

addition, an increase in quarterly employment growth lessens the recovery. This suggests that the impact of economic conditions is short-lived. In particular, the pattern of dip, drop and recovery of earnings loss can be explained by increased time out of work around the time of injury in poor economic conditions, but no increase in subsequent time out of work. After a certain amount of time, the impact of the local economic conditions at the time of injury seems to fade away, which appears in the model as improved recovery.

The results in the "All claims" row in Table 5.2 show an average across different groups that suggests that there is very little effect from economic conditions. However, the average may obscure the possibility that some groups are affected by economic conditions while others are not. Turning to the impact of economic conditions within severity group (the ratings groups shown in Table 5.2), we find that the only group for whom economic conditions affect losses to a significant extent (relative to the size of the losses) is the group with the lowest-rated claims. For ratings of 1 to 5, a 0.03 increase in quarterly employment growth would decrease the drop in earnings by three times $43.92, or approximately $132. This is approximately 10 percent of the average size of the drop reported in Table 5.1 ($1,364). A change of this size would also decrease the recovery for claims rated 1 to 5 by 16 percent, and therefore the long-term effects from economic conditions are likely to be less than ten percent. The more severe claims are negligibly affected by economic conditions. For instance, a three-percentage-point increase in quarterly employment growth decreases the drop for the most-severely disabled by approximately $84. This is less than 2.5 percent of the average drop for this severity group, as reported in Table 5.1. However, the relatively small effects on the more-severely injured may be more long lasting because the recovery is not at all affected by economic conditions.

Table 5.3 converts the numbers in Table 5.2 into the dollar change in losses over five years associated with a one-percentage-point increase in the employment growth rate. This summarizes the combined effect of economic conditions on dip, drop, and recovery. For the "All claims" group, a one-percentage-point increase in employment growth leads to a decline in losses over five years of $339.33. This is less than 1 percent of the total five-year earnings losses for PPD claimants over the five years after injury. This is clearly a small effect.

The largest effect of economic conditions is observed for the lowest-rated claims, those with disability ratings of 1 through 5. These workers are most likely to be accommodated by their employers and, if they leave the employer, they are also the most likely to be able to find another job given their (probably few) limitations. Over five years after injury, these workers experience a decline in earnings losses from a one-percentage-point increase in employment growth of $557.24, or 2.5 percent of their earnings losses over five years. Given a seven-percentage-point

Table 5.3

Change in Five-Year Earnings Losses Associated with a One-Percentage-Point Increase in Employment Growth

	Change in Losses ($)	Percentage Change
All claims	–339.33	–0.92
Rating 1–5	–557.24	–2.50
Rating 6–10	336.64	1.40
Rating 11–19	–14.99	–0.20
Rating 20–30	–664.94	–1.80
Rating 31–99	–500.12	–0.96

improvement in earnings losses from trough to peak of the business cycle, we would expect that the earnings losses for this group could decline by 17.5 percent.

The effects of employment growth on the other groups are smaller than for the least-severely injured. Indeed our estimate for the group of workers with the second-least severe injuries implies a *negative* effect from improving economic conditions. However, we should note that while the estimates for the second-least severely injured group indicate that economic conditions have a smaller statistically significant effect on them than on the least-severely injured group, the possibility of no effect from economic conditions on this group is also within the confidence interval of the estimates. Many of the differences across the severity groups are imprecisely estimated (see Reville and Schoeni, 2001).

We refer the reader to Reville and Schoeni (2001) for a discussion of differences across PPD claimants with different pre-injury earnings, industries, firms of different size, and different injuries.

CHAPTER 6

PREDICTING LOSSES FOR WORKERS INJURED IN MORE-RECENT YEARS

Because our earnings data are available only through the fourth quarter of 1998, we are only able to observe five-year earnings losses for workers who were injured no later than the fourth quarter of 1993. The primary goal of the analysis presented in this chapter was to construct a model that would allow us to estimate earnings losses for workers injured more recently than 1993. In addition, this chapter examines losses for workers employed in both insured and self-insured firms.

We use a multivariate statistical model, discussed in Chapter 5, which relates earnings losses to severity of injury, local economic conditions, and several other factors. This model was estimated in Chapter 5 using data on workers who were injured at insured firms in 1991 to 1995. In this chapter, we estimate the model using data on workers injured at self-insured firms, in addition to data on workers at insured firms. Both of these data sources are discussed in detail in the appendix.

In addition to controlling for employment growth rate, severity (as measured by disability ratings for workers at insured firms, and by total indemnity for workers at self-insured firms),[1] industry, and pre-injury earnings, we allow the effect of severity and pre-injury earnings to differ with the year of injury. By estimating separate models for workers at insured and self-insured firms, we also allow the effect of a disabling injury to differ for claimants at self-insured and insured firms in each year. Using the estimates from the models, we then predicted losses at five and ten years using all claims from the WCIRB data[2] and data on the self-insured claims from the sample collected by RAND and described in Reville et al. (2001). In this chapter, we combine the self-insured and insured employer estimates into statewide figures by weighting the self-insured

---

[1]The estimate of severity for claimants at insured firms is based on disability rating groups that are approximately in quintiles (with a breakdown of the ratings distribution at every twentieth percentile). Specifically, we use ratings of 1 to 5, 6 to 10, 11 to 20, 21 to 35, and 36 to 99. For the self-insured claimants, because ratings are unavailable in our data, we used quintiles of total disability instead. The breakpoints for total disability are $3,914, $9,356, $18,263, and $36,648.

[2]These estimates were based on the total sample of claims, including claims that were not matched to comparison workers, thus representing the full population of insured claims. The average value for the level of claim closing in the simulations is set to its 1994 level instead of the level observed in the WCIRB-EDD (Employment Development Department) matched data. This eliminates the effect of undersampling of early closing claims due to missing Social Security numbers, which is discussed further in the appendix.

estimates to constitute 21 percent of the sample, which was the percentage of workers' compensation claims from self-insured firms in the early 1990s.

Estimates of losses beyond the observed period are calculated by assuming that the rate of recovery that is estimated during the observed period continues until 20 quarters (five years) or 40 quarters (ten years) after injury. (The number of observations used in the model-based predictions is reported in the appendix.) We also used information on indemnity incurred (or paid-for claims at insured firms when incurred amounts were unavailable) to calculate replacement rates. For indemnity, we included temporary disability, PPD, and the vocational rehabilitation maintenance allowance.[3] We estimated indemnity at five years, accounting for the effect of accelerated payments through compromise and release agreements and the use of incurred instead of paid amounts (see Reville et al. [2001] for more details). We used the full amount of indemnity that was reported for the ten-year estimates.

The simulated estimates for injuries occurring in 1996 and 1997 were derived by using WCIRB claims data for those two years and the earnings loss estimates from the 1991 to 1995 injury-year data. We do not have claims data for 1996 and 1997 on injured workers at self-insured firms; therefore, for those workers, the 1995 estimates are carried forward. We do not have wage data for workers injured at insured firms in 1996 and 1997 and therefore the estimates for workers at insured firms are based only on the claims information. In addition to wages, other variables, such as industry, that are used in the estimation are unavailable from the claims data for 1996 and 1997. The value used in the simulation for these unavailable variables is also carried forward from 1995. Because county of injury is unavailable from the claims data, a weighted employment growth rate is constructed using actual 1996 and 1997 California county employment growth rates and distribution of injuries by county from the data for 1995. Essentially, the 1996 and 1997 estimates are based on 1995 data, but we used actual insured claims for 1996 and 1997 to calculate replacement rates. We estimated losses using injury severity (as measured by disability ratings), pre-injury average weekly earnings observed in 1996 and 1997, and economic conditions in the state during those years.

Table 6.1 reports the results of the simulation of earnings losses at five and ten years for PPD claimants injured in 1991 to 1997. The simulations for workers injured in 1991 to 1995 confirm the losses reported in Chapter 4 that were not based on the simulation procedures. That is, wage losses declined after 1991, a decline that ended in 1994. Workers with PPDs who were injured in 1991 had five-year earnings losses (before benefits are paid) of $36,334; those losses

---

[3]For the claims from workers at self-insured firms, in some cases we were not able to distinguish vocational rehabilitation training and evaluation payments from maintenance allowance. In these cases, we included the full amount of vocational rehabilitation as indemnity.

Table 6.1

Predicted Earnings Losses and Replacement Rates

Year of Injury	Predicted Earnings Losses ($)	Benefits ($)	Before-Tax Replacement Rates	After-Tax Replacement Rates
		Five Years After Injury (20 Quarters)		
1991	36,334	18,934	0.52	0.68
1992	32,716	18,994	0.58	0.75
1993	33,253	18,490	0.56	0.72
1994	31,761	18,169	0.57	0.74
1995	33,619	19,106	0.57	0.74
1996	33,716	19,747	0.59	0.76
1997	33,572	19,629	0.58	0.76
		Ten Years After Injury (40 Quarters)		
1991	53,113	22,705	0.43	0.56
1992	47,450	22,913	0.48	0.63
1993	49,896	22,584	0.45	0.59
1994	46,929	21,609	0.46	0.60
1995	50,623	22,460	0.44	0.58
1996	50,945	23,791	0.47	0.61
1997	50,502	22,987	0.46	0.59

declined to $31,761 for workers injured in 1994. Ten-year losses were $53,113 for workers injured in 1991, and those losses declined to a low of $46,929 for workers injured in 1994.[4]

Benefits (in real-inflation-corrected terms) are also observed as declining somewhat through 1994, and subsequently increasing through 1997 as the 1993 benefit increases took effect in phases. The result is that the before-tax replacement rates over the five years steadily increase over the 1990s, to approximately 0.58 by 1997. After-tax replacement rates[5] at five years (reported because workers' compensation benefits are tax-free) increase from 0.68 to 0.76 by 1997. Replacement rates are lower ten years after injury because while earnings losses continue beyond five years, benefits continue beyond five years for only less than 20 percent of workers. Before-tax replacement rates ten years after injury increase from 0.43 for workers injured in 1991 to 0.46 for workers injured in 1997. After-tax replacement rates ten years after injury increase from 0.56 in 1991 to 0.59 in 1997.[6]

---

[4]It is worth noting that the 1991 estimates of wage losses are lower and the replacement rates are higher than the estimates in Peterson et al. (1998) and in Chapter 4. This discrepancy occurs because the statistical analysis corrects for the data limitations, specifically with regard to late-closing claims.

[5]In Reville et al. (2001), after-tax losses were calculated for each injured worker. In general, those losses led to after-tax estimates of losses that are approximately 77 percent of the before-tax estimates. This general rule was adopted here to calculate after-tax replacement rates.

[6]The estimates for 1996 and 1997 use data from at least 30 months after injury. However, the incurred benefits that are reported by insurers to the WCIRB may still increase after 30 months. Thus, after

As stated earlier in this report, the standard for judging the adequacy of workers' compensation indemnity benefits is two-thirds replacement of pre-tax losses (Berkowitz and Burton, 1987). This standard is based on the wage replacement rate associated with temporary disability benefits. For PPD benefits, the time period over which this standard is intended to apply is uncertain: Is it five years, ten years, a lifetime, or some other time period? If the time period is ten years, California falls far short of the two-thirds replacement standard, not achieving even a one-half replacement rate. If the standard is five years, California's benefits are still inadequate, although over the 1990s, between declining wage losses and increasing benefits, the system has come closer to achieving adequacy.

We extended the simulations to examine the differences in losses and replacement rates by severity of injury. Because the data combine claims from both self-insured and insured firms, and extend to 1997, this allows us to examine equity of benefits using the most comprehensive data on losses available to date.[7]

Table 6.2 reports simulations of five-year earnings losses, benefits, and pre-tax replacement rates for 1991 through 1997, by severity (as measured by disability rating). Table 6.3 reports ten-year losses, benefits, and pre-tax replacement rates by disability rating for the same period. Table 6.2 and Table 6.3 reveal a pattern that was observed previously and discussed in both Peterson et al. (1998) and Reville et al. (2001)—the replacement rates are lowest for the least severe injuries. This occurs because the least severe injuries receive relatively low benefits on the assumption that the injuries do not result in significant impairment. For instance, these injuries may involve the loss of a finger, or relatively minor (although permanent) back injuries. Nonetheless, these lesser-impairment injuries seem to result in significant and sustained economic losses that substantially exceed the dollars paid in benefits.

At the same time that Table 6.2 reveals low replacement rates for lower-rated claims, it also shows dramatic improvements occurring for the lowest and second-lowest severity rating groups. Earnings losses declined from $24,156 to $15,254 for the lowest severity group, those with disability ratings of 1 to 5; and declined from $25,137 to $18,995 for the second-lowest

---

30 months, both the reported severity of the injury and the reported total benefits paid may increase for open claims. The impact of higher benefits after 30 months (the numerator) and higher severity rating (the denominator) on the replacement rate is uncertain.

[7]The data imposed some limitations on our analysis. For severity, in particular, disability ratings were used for the insured claimants and total indemnity was used for the self-insured claimants. This limitation did not pose a problem in the overall estimates because the losses were calculated separately by insurance status for each quintile of severity. However, when combining quintiles, we are not necessarily combining self-insured and insured claimants with the same injury severity in each quintile. We have experimented with several different specifications from the ones reported here, and the results are not qualitatively different.

Table 6.2

Five-Year Cumulative Earnings Losses, Benefits, Pre-Tax Replacement Rates, and Uncompensated Earnings Losses by Severity and Year of Injury

	Severity (Rating)	1991	1992	1993	1994	1995	1996	1997
Cumulative earnings losses ($)	1–5	24,156	20,849	17,804	15,972	15,041	15,408	15,254
Benefits ($)		3,487	3,467	3,070	3,016	3,336	3,308	3,465
Replacement rate		0.14	0.17	0.17	0.19	0.22	0.21	0.23
Uncompensated earnings losses ($)		20,669	17,382	14,734	12,956	11,705	12,100	11,789
Cumulative earnings losses ($)	6–10	25,137	20,620	16,694	14,505	18,079	18,566	18,995
Benefits ($)		7,545	7,117	6,675	6,710	6,591	7,280	7,448
Replacement rate		0.30	0.35	0.40	0.46	0.36	0.39	0.39
Uncompensated earnings losses ($)		17,592	13,503	10,019	7,795	11,488	11,286	11,547
Cumulative earnings losses ($)	11–20	28,720	25,183	25,659	23,144	24,649	24,498	24,732
Benefits ($)		14,342	13,846	13,330	12,754	13,435	14,383	14,458
Replacement rate		0.50	0.55	0.52	0.55	0.55	0.59	0.58
Uncompensated earnings losses ($)		14,378	11,337	12,329	10,391	11,214	10,115	10,274
Cumulative earnings losses ($)	21–35	45,171	37,816	41,033	40,533	40,118	39,495	39,624
Benefits ($)		28,410	27,541	25,793	25,557	26,847	28,129	28,303
Replacement rate		0.63	0.73	0.63	0.63	0.67	0.71	0.71
Uncompensated earnings losses ($)		16,761	10,275	15,240	14,976	13,271	11,365	11,321
Cumulative earnings losses ($)	36–99	68,804	68,807	67,590	68,025	73,004	73,925	73,210
Benefits ($)		47,215	46,747	43,705	43,714	45,144	44,661	44,212
Replacement rate		0.69	0.68	0.65	0.64	0.62	0.60	0.60
Uncompensated earnings losses ($)		21,590	22,061	23,885	24,311	27,860	29,264	28,998

severity group, those with disability ratings of 6 to 10. As a result, pre-tax replacement rates at five years for the 1-to-5 disability-rating group increased from 14 percent in 1991 to 22 percent by 1995. This improvement in replacement rates is remarkable because it occurred without any statutory change in benefits.

Similarly, pre-tax five-year replacement rates for the second-lowest severity group increased from 0.30 in 1991 to 0.39 by 1997. Earnings losses declined from $28,720 in 1991 to $24,732 in 1997 for the third most-severely injured group, those with disability ratings of 11 to 20. The 11-to-20 rating group's average replacement rate increased from 0.50 in 1991 to about 0.58 in 1997. In Table 6.3, similar improvements in pre-tax replacement rates are observed at ten years for all three groups. The replacement rate rose from 0.10 to 0.13 for the group with the least severe injuries, rose from 0.21 to 0.30 for the group with the second most-severe injuries, and rose from 0.37 to 0.46 for the group with the third most-severe injuries.

Improvements in outcomes for workers in the lower-rated injury-severity groups do not appear to have been driven by economic conditions, as discussed in Chapter 5. Although we have no data to test this hypothesis, we suspect that the increased use of return-to-work programs over the 1990s (driven by higher insurance rates over the decade, increased awareness of return to work as a strategy for lowering workers' compensation costs, and perhaps also the ADA) may have driven this improvement. Injured workers with lower-severity claims are the most easily accommodated because their lesser impairments would lead to fewer limitations in terms of employment in the workplace.

The second-highest severity group, those with disability ratings of 21 to 35, experienced a decline in earnings losses at five-years, from $45,171 for a worker injured in 1991 to $39,624 for a worker injured in 1997, and an increase in the wage replacement rate, which went from 0.63 to 0.71 (as shown in Table 6.2). At ten years (as shown in Table 6.3), pre-tax replacement rates increased from 0.46 for a worker injured in 1991 to 0.55 for a worker injured in 1997.

Workers in the highest injury-severity group, those with disability ratings from 36 to 99, do not appear to have experienced any reduction in earnings losses between 1991 and 1997. Indeed, losses are observed to be higher for those injured in 1995 than for those injured in 1991. In addition, total benefits over time appear to have decreased somewhat for this group. The decline in the reported benefits paid in the 1996 and 1997 estimates may be driven by the relative immaturity of the claims, but the 1995 estimates are likely to be fully mature.[8] The increase in earnings losses for the group with the most-severe injuries is therefore quite striking.

As noted in Chapter 2, a growing amount of literature has documented declining employment among the disabled during the 1990s (Acemoglu and Angrist, 2001; Deleire, 2000; Bound and Waidmann, 2000; Burkhauser et al., 2000). Among the workers' compensation population, the definition of disability, as used in these articles, is most applicable to workers in the highest injury-severity group. The results in this report are consistent with the findings in those articles—the outcomes for the severely disabled did not improve over the 1990s. Despite improvements due to economic conditions and increased use of return-to-work programs that appear to have led to improvements in outcomes for the other injury-severity groups, the first half of the 1990s saw no improvement or some deterioration in outcomes for the most severely injured workers.

---

[8]Only claims from the 1994 policy year are used for the 1995 estimates.

Table 6.3

Ten-Year Cumulative Earnings Losses, Benefits, Pre-Tax Replacement Rates, and Uncompensated Earnings Losses by Severity and Year of Injury

	Severity (Rating)	1991	1992	1993	1994	1995	1996	1997
Cumulative earnings losses ($)	1–5	34,240	27,293	23,401	22,414	25,268	26,792	26,313
Benefits ($)		3,524	3,524	3,074	3,028	3,371	3,369	3,518
Replacement rate		0.10	0.13	0.13	0.14	0.13	0.13	0.13
Uncompensated earnings losses ($)		30,715	23,769	20,327	19,386	21,898	23,423	22,795
Cumulative earnings losses ($)	6–10	36,267	24,696	20,320	17,016	22,741	24,050	25,096
Benefits ($)		7,599	7,228	6,686	6,733	6,593	7,368	7,537
Replacement rate		0.21	0.29	0.33	0.40	0.29	0.31	0.30
Uncompensated earnings losses ($)		28,669	17,469	13,634	10,283	16,148	16,682	17,559
Cumulative earnings losses ($)	11–20	39,496	33,830	34,601	29,689	31,917	31,425	31,737
Benefits ($)		14,481	14,146	13,406	12,871	13,489	14,571	14,622
Replacement rate		0.37	0.42	0.39	0.43	0.42	0.46	0.46
Uncompensated earnings losses ($)		25,015	19,684	21,195	16,818	18,428	16,854	17,115
Cumulative earnings losses ($)	21–35	64,474	53,135	63,095	59,713	53,981	53,205	53,431
Benefits ($)		29,967	28,731	26,554	26,322	27,340	29,594	29,504
Replacement rate		0.46	0.54	0.42	0.44	0.51	0.56	0.55
Uncompensated earnings losses ($)		34,507	24,404	36,542	33,391	26,641	23,611	23,927
Cumulative earnings losses ($)	36–99	109,716	118,605	114,178	121,672	127,127	129,659	128,046
Benefits ($)		68,717	68,335	65,711	62,247	62,767	65,848	62,542
Replacement rate		0.63	0.58	0.58	0.51	0.49	0.51	0.49
Uncompensated earnings losses ($)		40,999	50,269	48,468	59,425	64,360	63,811	65,504

Tables 6.2 and 6.3 also report *uncompensated earnings losses,* which are the earnings losses that remain after benefits are paid. We have noted that the workers with the least severe injuries have the lowest replacement rates, suggesting that benefits are not equitable. When evaluating equity of benefits by severity group, it is worthwhile to consider the uncompensated earnings losses as well.

By 1997, uncompensated earnings losses at five years for the least severely injured had declined from more than $20,000 to less than $12,000. At the same time, uncompensated losses for the most severely injured had increased from $21,590 to nearly $29,000. In 1991, the two groups had comparable uncompensated losses but very different replacement rates, which would have suggested that benefit increases should be targeted toward those workers with the least severe injuries. By 1997, replacement rates increased for the least severely injured workers. Given the significant uncompensated losses of the most severely injured, targeting benefits to the least severely injured is less compelling than it was. It is possible that improved return-to-work programs are the most appropriate way to improve outcomes for the least severely injured workers, whereas increased benefits is the best way to improve outcomes for the most severely injured ones.

CHAPTER 7

CONCLUSIONS

Over the early 1990s, large declines were observed in earnings losses for permanent partial disability claimants in California. The largest declines in earnings losses are observed for the lowest-rated claims (claims with disability ratings below 10.0, and especially claims with ratings below 5.0). We investigated whether these results are related to the improved economic conditions in California after the recession of the early 1990s. We find that while local economic conditions at the time of injury have *some* impact on the longer-term losses experienced by PPD claimants, most of the overall downward trend in earnings losses during the study period cannot be traced to changes in the state's economic situation.

The patterns in earnings losses may be more closely related to conditions in the workers' compensation market during the early 1990s. In particular, prior to 1993 when workers' compensation reform legislation was enacted, claims frequency and insurance rates had increased dramatically. Since 1993, those rates have fallen. (Both the largest increases and the largest declines in claims frequency and insurance rates in California were observed at firms located in the Los Angeles basin.) The same general pattern also is observed for earnings losses. It is possible that the earnings losses in the early 1990s reflected a system in crisis and its impact on injured workers. As firms were overwhelmed with claims, the ability to accommodate workers with injuries in a manner that minimized losses may have been compromised. Since that time, in response to the increased insurance rates experienced during the early 1990s, firms have adopted procedures to improve the rate of return to sustained work for injured employees, the result being lower earnings losses. Although this explanation is in accordance with the patterns observed and reported on in this report, we leave testing of this hypothesis to future research.

As part of our study, we used a statistical model to predict earnings losses five and ten years after injury for workers injured from 1991 through 1997 in California. The model was estimated and losses were predicted using data from both self-insured and insured firms. The results suggest that whereas replacement rates of five-year losses had improved for PPD claimants during the mid-1990s, the replacement rates remained below 60 percent of pre-injury earnings. Replacement rates of ten-year losses were lower still, remaining below one-half of pre-injury earnings.

These estimates suggest that although benefit levels have increased since 1991 and earnings losses have declined, outcomes did not improve with better economic conditions over later years and replacement rates still remain below the two-thirds wage-replacement standard commonly cited for adequacy. In addition, because the economy appears to be headed toward a recession as of late 2001, and benefits have remained fixed in nominal terms since 1996 (declining in real terms due to inflation), we may expect that even though the effect from current economic conditions is not large, outcomes for workers who are injured today will be worse than the outcomes we observed for workers in 1996 to 1997.

Differences across groups of employees who have injuries of differing severity suggest that the improvement in outcomes is greater for claimants with less-severe injuries. In fact, claimants with the most-severe injuries (those with the highest-rated claims) experienced no change in their outcomes over the study period. This result is surprising because it was the higher-rated claims that received PPD increases with the 1993 workers' compensation reform legislation. However, we suspect that less-disabled claimants (those with lower-rated claims) are more readily accommodated by their employers, enabling them to return to work more quickly.

The improving economy, combined with increased return-to-work programs, allowed less-disabled workers to experience improved outcomes during the 1990s despite PPD benefit levels that remained stable. In addition, TTD benefits increased after 1993 and workers with lower-rated claims have a higher fraction of their total indemnity paid in TTD benefits than do workers with higher-rated claims. In contrast, the outcomes for injured workers with higher-rated claims are consistent with the literature (including Acemoglu and Angrist, 2001; Deleire, 2000; and Bound and Waidmann, 2000) that has described a decline in employment among disabled workers during the 1990s.

APPENDIX

DATA SOURCES AND ANALYSIS SAMPLES

Our data on the earnings and benefits paid to PPD claimants are drawn from two sources, one for workers injured at firms that purchase insurance for workers' compensation (insured employers) and one for workers injured at self-insured employers. In Chapter 5, where we discuss the impact of economic conditions at the time of injury on long-term outcomes for disabled workers, we summarize and interpret analyses from Reville and Schoeni (2001). That document includes data from insured employers only because a wider range of variables is available on the insured database. In Chapter 6, we used the models developed for Reville and Schoeni (2001) to provide overall statewide estimates of earnings losses and replacement rates, at five and ten years after injury, for workers injured in 1991 through 1997. The estimates in Chapter 6 combine insured employer data with self-insured employer data.

For insured employers, we analyzed claims from 1991 through 1995 using a database maintained by the WCIRB. The claims records from the WCIRB database were linked to quarterly wage data for claimants at every employer in California, which were obtained from a database supplied by the California EDD. We also identified the injured employees' comparison workers using the same EDD database. The EDD also supplied data on earnings, for both injured and comparison workers, at all California employers for several years before and after injury. As shown in Table A.1, the database includes 31,077 workers at insured firms who were injured between the first quarter of 1991[1] and the fourth quarter of 1995. Those injured workers were matched to 108,164 controls. A detailed discussion of these data is available in Peterson et al. (1998) and in Reville and Schoeni (2001).[2]

[1]Data are available from only the second quarter of 1991 for self-insured employers.

[2]There are two primary limitations to this database, as discussed further in Peterson et al. (1998) and Reville and Schoeni (2001). First, approximately one-third of injured workers did not have comparison workers. Those workers without controls typically work at small firms where there are so few other workers to choose from that a sample of comparison workers is simply not available. But this lack of comparison workers also reflects a reduction in data extracted by the EDD due to the complexity of manipulating the EDD wage file. Second, claims from injury years 1991 through 1993 overrepresent late-closing claims. This overrepresentation resulted because the WCIRB did not require insurers to report Social Security numbers until the 1993 policy year (which represents half the claims from injury years 1993 and 1994), and claims from earlier years include Social Security numbers only if the claims were still open at the time of the 1993 policy year reports from insurers to the WCIRB. We correct for both of these limitations in the estimates in Chapter 6.

Table A.1

Sample Sizes by Year of Injury and Insurance Status

	Model Estimates			
Year of Injury	Claimants at Insured Employers	Claimants at Self-Insured Employers	Pooled Claimants	Simulation Estimates
1991	6,286	3,993[a]	10,279	13,608
1992	5,949	4,565	10,514	13,450
1993	7,792	4,242	12,034	15,868
1994	8,292	4,413	12,705	16,877
1995	2,758	4,049	6,807	8,145
1996	—	—	—	77,610
1997	—	—	—	30,880
Total	31,077	21,262	52,339	176,438

[a]Data are available from only the second quarter of 1991 on for self-insured employers.

For self-insured employers, we used workers' compensation claims data that were collected and assembled into a database by RAND. The self-insured employer data came solely from private firms. As with the insured-employer data, these data were linked to EDD data to create longitudinal records on wages and employment for all injured workers. Longitudinal data on wages for comparison workers were drawn from the injured workers' employers through the EDD data. Comparison workers at self-insured firms are selected in the same manner as comparison workers at insured firms except that they are matched to the injured worker on the basis of their tenure at the firm as well as their pre-injury wages.

As shown in Table A.1, we obtained data on 21,262 workers with PPD claims at self-insured employers. A detailed discussion of this database is available in Reville et al. (2001). In the estimates shown in Chapter 6, which pool self-insured and insured claimants, the self-insured claimants are weighted to represent 21 percent of the sample, which is the fraction of the population of claimants working for self-insured employers.

In Chapter 6, we report estimates of simulations that correct for several deficiencies in the data, as described in Footnote 3. Those simulations also include projections of losses for workers injured in 1996 and 1997. The numbers of observations in the data used for the simulations are reported in the far-right column of Table A.1. These are the most comprehensive and up-to-date estimates of outcomes for PPD claimants in California that are available as of late 2001. More than 176,000 individuals with PPD claims are included in the simulation estimates.

All wages are converted into 1997 dollars using the West Region Consumer Price Index published by the U.S. Department of Labor Bureau of Labor Statistics. Benefits are also converted to real dollars under the assumption that they are paid at two years after the injury date.

The observations were divided by county in order to measure local economic conditions. Because the sample sizes in a number of counties were not large enough to accurately estimate earnings loss, we grouped together some counties. These groupings are based on geography and similarity in patterns of earnings. The 13 individual counties or county groups are listed in Table A.2.

Table A.2

California Counties and County Groupings

Alameda	**North** (cont.)	**San Bernadino**
	Mendocino	
Central Coast	Modoc	**San Diego**
San Luis Obispo	Plumas	
Santa Barbara	Shasta	**San Francisco**
Ventura	Siskiyou	Contra Costa
	Sutter	Marin
Fresno	Tehama	Napa
Fresno	Trinity	San Francisco
Kern	Yuba	San Mateo
Kings		Santa Cruz
Madera	**Orange**	Solano
Mariposa		Sonoma
Merced	**Riverside**	
Monterey	Imperial	**San Joaquin**
San Benito	Riverside	Calaveras
Tulare		Inyo
	Sacramento	Mono
Los Angeles	Alpine	San Joaquin
	Amador	Stanislaus
North	Colusa	Tuolumne
Butte	El Dorado	
Del Norte	Nevada	**Santa Clara**
Glenn	Placer	
Humboldt	Sacramento	
Lake	Sierra	
Lassen	Yolo	

REFERENCES

Acemoglu, Daron, and Joshua D. Angrist, "Consequences of Employment Protection: The Case of the Americans with Disabilities Act," *Journal of Political Economy*, Vol. 109, No. 5, pp. 915–957, 2001.

Berkowitz, Monroe, and John F. Burton, Jr., *Permanent Disability Benefits in Workers' Compensation*, Kalamazoo, Mich.: W. E. Upjohn Institute for Employment Research, 1987.

Bound, John, and Timothy Waidmann, "Accounting for Recent Declines in Employment Rates Among the Working-Aged Disabled," NBER Working Paper 7975, Cambridge, Mass.: National Bureau of Economic Research, 2000.

Burkhauser, Richard V., Mary C. Daly, and Andrew J. Houtenville, "How Working Age People with Disabilities Fared over the 1990s Business Cycle," in Peter Budetti, Janice Gregory, and Richard Burkhauser, eds., *Ensuring Health and Income Security for an Aging Work Force*, Kalamazoo, Mich.: W. E. Upjohn Institute for Employment Research, 2000.

CHSWC Annual Report, 1999–2000, State of California Department of Industrial Relations, San Francisco, July 2000.

Deleire, Thomas, "The Wage and Employment Effects of the Americans with Disabilities Act," *Journal of Human Resources*, Vol. 35, No. 4, pp. 693–715, 2000.

Efron, Bradley, and Robert J. Tibshirani, *An Introduction to the Bootstrap,* London, England: Chapman and Hall, 1993.

Meyer, Bruce D., W. Kip Viscusi, and David L. Durbin, "Workers' Compensation and Injury Duration: Evidence from a Natural Experiment," *The American Economic Review,* Vol. 85, No. 3, pp. 322–340, 1995.

Peterson, Mark, Robert T. Reville, Rachel Kaganoff Stern, and Peter S. Barth, *Compensating Permanent Workplace Injuries: A Study of the California System,* Santa Monica, Calif.: RAND, MR-920-ICJ, 1998.

Reville, Robert T., Suzanne Polich, Seth Seabury, and Elizabeth Giddens, *Permanent Disability at Private Self-Insured Firms: A Study of Earnings Loss, Replacement, and Return to Work for Workers' Compensation Claimants,* Santa Monica, Calif.: RAND, MR-1268-ICJ, 2001.

Reville, Robert T., and Robert F. Schoeni, *Disability from Injuries at Work: The Effect on Earnings and Employment*, RAND Labor and Population Program Working Paper Series 01–08, Santa Monica, Calif.: RAND, DRU-2554-ICJ, 2001.